P9-CCD-817

Sunset
Lawns & Ground Covers

**By the Editors of Sunset Books
and Sunset Magazine**

Lane Publishing Co., Menlo Park, California

Acknowledgments

We appreciate the help of the following lawn
and ground cover experts in the preparation
of this book: Wayne Austin, Agronomist,
Orinda, California; George S. Kido, Regional
Editor, *Lawn Care Magazine*, Oakland,
California; Carl S. Koehler, Urban Pest Manage-
ment Specialist, University of California,
Berkeley; Arthur H. McCain, Extension Plant
Pathologist, University of California, Berkeley;
Carl R. Martin, Product Manager, Agricultural
Chemical Products, Kalamazoo, Michigan;
James C. Perry, Nurseryman, La Puente, Cali-
fornia; Richard W. Smiley, Assistant Professor
of Plant Pathology, Cornell University, Ithaca,
New York; Stan Spaulding, Staff Research
Associate, Department of Botany and Plant
Sciences, University of California, Riverside.
Also, our thanks to Philip Edinger and
Will Kirkman for special editorial assistance.

Edited by Kathryn L. Arthurs

Special Consultants: Joseph F. Williamson
Garden Editor, *Sunset* Magazine
John R. Dunmire
Associate Editor, *Sunset* Magazine

Design: Terrence Meagher

Illustrations: Mike Valdez

Cover: Well-groomed, cool-season lawn contrasts
nicely with the ground cover plantings that border
it. Ground covers include hedera (top left—see
description on page 73), junipers (lower right—see
description on page 79), and ice plant (lower left
corner—see description on pages 74, 79). Photo-
graphed by Steve W. Marley.

Sunset Books
  Editor, David E. Clark
  Managing Editor, Elizabeth L. Hogan
Seventh printing November 1987

Copyright © 1979, 1964, 1960, 1955, Lane Publishing Co., Menlo Park,
CA 94025. Fourth edition. World rights reserved. No part of this
publication may be reproduced by any mechanical, photographic, or
electronic process, or in the form of a phonographic recording, nor
may it be stored in a retrieval system, transmitted, or otherwise
copied for public or private use without prior written permission
from the publisher. Library of Congress Number: 78-70267. ISBN
0-376-03507-2. Lithographed in the United States.

Contents

Lawns   4-37

Ground Covers   38-95

Index   96

Special Features

Lawns

A Basic Landscape Element

Lawns are for people. No other surface feels so good
under bare feet or works as well for a game of croquet or
touch football or for children to run and tumble on.
No other surface can be kept looking consistently good with
just watering, mowing, and trimming. In short,
no other surface—whether it's paving, low-growing ground
covers, or artificial turf—can really replace a well-cared-for lawn.
This section contains from-the-ground-up information
on how to plant and maintain the type of lawn that's best
for you. It includes the latest thinking on new types
of lawn grasses and lawn care products, as well as how
to deal with problems.

Good Soil Is Basic

Good soil is essential to a healthy lawn. Once grass is established, you can aerate and fertilize it, but the actual soil base can't be reworked. If you carefully prepare the soil layer in the beginning, your lawn can start with a good foundation.

What Type Soil Do You Have?

Soils come in two basic types: clay or sandy. Heavy soil, called clay or adobe, is easy to recognize but difficult to work with. If you squeeze a handful together, you'll get a gummy plastic mass that won't break apart even if you tap it with a shovel. Though clay soil is often rich in nutrients, it contains very little space for air; grass roots may refuse to grow because of the lack of oxygen, and often they drown because of poor drainage. Clay soils do have an advantage: slow drainage through tiny, compacted particles prevents nutrients from leaching out.

Sandy soil, on the other hand, has huge particles that allow good aeration, quick passage of water, and rapid temperature change. Sandy soil provides plenty of air for plant roots, and the roots can spread easily. But here's the rub: water will pour right through the soil, taking with it any soluble plant nutrients you've applied.

Soil Amendments

To improve your soil quality, you can add mineral or organic amendments. Mineral amendments come in small-chunk form. Added to fine, heavy soil, they stay in place more or less permanently. Sand, perlite, pumice, and vermiculite are examples of mineral amendments. Most of these materials are too expensive to be considered for improving large areas.

Organic amendments are almost anything that comes originally from an animal or plant, such as bone meal, peat moss, leaf mold, or manure. These materials improve dense clay soils by physically separating clay particles.

To improve sandy soils, you should add a spongy amendment such as peat moss. Spongy particles fill the spaces between sand particles, helping the soil retain moisture and nutrients.

Some organic materials are primarily a source of nutrients and are normally used as fertilizer; an example is bone meal which is rich in phosphorus. Other organics contain no nutrients but help fluff up heavy soil and then rot to produce humus; peat moss is this type of amendment. Some contain tiny amounts of plant nutrients, such as manures, but are used mainly to improve soil texture. Organic amendments are discussed on page 6.

When you add an amendment, the final soil mixture should be about ⅓ amendment and ⅔ soil. If your soil is almost pure clay or sand, the finished mix should be ½ amendment and ½ soil. Work in the amendments with a spade or rotary tiller to a depth of 9

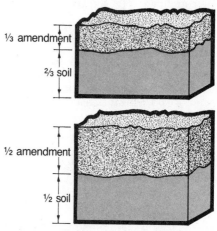

For normal soil (top), final mix should be ⅓ amendment; for clay soil (lower), ½ amendment.

inches; apply a 2 to 3-inch layer of amendment over the soil (use a 4 to 5-inch layer for a half-and-half mixture), then cultivate thoroughly.

If you plan to add fertilizers at this point, see pages 16–17.

Special Soil Problems

If your garden seems to perform poorly despite good care, you may have a special soil problem. If you suspect this, you may want to have the soil tested before you plant a lawn.

You can test the soil yourself with a soil-testing kit (check at your local garden center or look in a seed catalog) or send a soil sample to a testing laboratory for professional analysis. Dig up trowel-size samples from the top 6 inches of soil from widely scattered spots throughout the lawn area. Mix the samples together thoroughly, then retain about a pint of the mixed

(Continued on next page)

Soil Types and Sizes

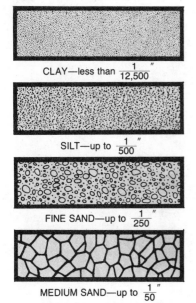

CLAY—less than $\frac{1}{12,500}''$

SILT—up to $\frac{1}{500}''$

FINE SAND—up to $\frac{1}{250}''$

MEDIUM SAND—up to $\frac{1}{50}''$

LARGEST SAND PARTICLE—up to $\frac{1}{12}''$

soil for testing. To find a soil-testing lab, check the Yellow Pages of your phone book under "Laboratories—Testing" or ask your County Cooperative Extension Advisor (or agricultural advisor) for a local laboratory.

Following is a list of soil problems with possible solutions:

Alkalinity. Alkaline soil, common in light-rainfall areas, is high in calcium carbonate (lime) and other minerals. Many plants grow well in moderately alkaline soil, though acid-loving plants do not. Gypsum, which has the advantage of practically limitless safe application, can be added to the soil to lessen the alkalinity. Spread it on the top of the soil—directions usually say "like a light snow"—and spade it in. This is about 35 to 50 pounds of gypsum per 1,000 square feet of soil.

Acidity. Acid soil is most common in heavy-rainfall areas. Since all acid soils have low levels of calcium (lime), ground limestone will help neutralize an acid-reacting soil. If you do add lime, use a fertilizer that won't increase soil acidity (check the label).

Salinity. This condition is a widespread problem in arid and semiarid regions. A high concentration of salts in the root zone area can prevent seed germination, stunt plant growth, and turn grasses yellow or brown—a condition known as salt burn. If Bermuda, a salt tolerant grass, shows salt injury, then lawns have no place here.

Periodic and thorough leaching will lessen the salt content. To leach a turf area, let a hose or soaker (see pages 13 and 39) run at a slow trickle for several hours, moving it around the lawn to completely leach the area.

Chlorosis. If you've fertilized properly and the grass turns yellow, the soil may be deficient in iron—a condition known as chlorosis. Chelating (pronounced *key*-lating) agents or iron sulfate can control chlorosis; buy them either at a nursery or garden supply center. Follow label directions exactly.

Shallow soil or hardpan. A layer of hardpan (hard, claylike matter under soft soil), within the top 18 inches of your soil stops water penetration and inhibits root growth. To counteract this condition, you can drill through shallow hardpan to make a vertical drain or get advice from an engineer on how to install drain tiles horizontally.

Manmade hardpan exists where heavy construction equipment has compacted soil, making claylike sub-soil brick-hard when dried. To remedy this condition, you can grow a crop of deep-rooted grass—annual rye, for example—and plow it under before adding amendments.

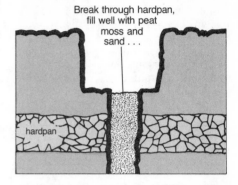

Break through hardpan, fill well with peat moss and sand . . .

hardpan

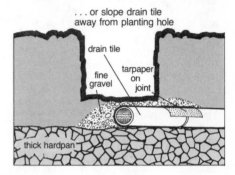

. . . or slope drain tile away from planting hole

drain tile

fine gravel

tarpaper on joint

thick hardpan

Organic Soil Amendments

Organic soil amendments are used to improve soil either by serving as fertilizers and adding nutrients to the soil (bone meal is rich in phosphorus) or by fluffing up heavy soil and then rotting to produce humus (peat moss is of this type). An organic amendment may be almost anything that is an animal or plant by-product.

What to Look For

While there are several important considerations in choosing a soil amendment, the most important one is its texture. If possible, choose an amendment that is granular and fine-grained; granular materials are easier to mix into soil evenly than fibrous materials. And even-textured materials amend soil better than variable ones.

Salt content is another consideration in choice of a soil amendment. If you live in an area that receives normal rainfall, some salt content in the amendment will cause little if any problem. But if your region has little rainfall, the salt content could be crucial. Without heavy rains to wash away salts, young or sensitive plants could be burned. The amount of ash (mineral matter) an amendment contains affects its usefulness. Ash is of questionable value in improving soil, and the higher the percentage, the less efficient the product.

Some materials, such as sawdust or ground bark, decompose quickly, using up valuable nitrogen. You'll need to add extra nitrogen along with these conditioners; see page 16 for information.

The amendments listed below are all useful, but availability will vary by area.

• Redwood products: granular or granular-fibrous; low salt, ash; long lasting; add ⅓ pound actual nitrogen per 10 cubic feet of lawn.
• Bark: granular; low salt, ash; long lasting; very dense material; add 1 pound actual nitrogen per 10 cubic feet.
• Fir sawdust: granular; low salt, ash; long lasting; add ½ pound actual nitrogen per 10 cubic feet. DO NOT USE PINE SAWDUST.
• Hypnum peat moss: fibrous; high in ash; needs no added nitrogen.
• Sedge peat: fibrous; texture variable; may be saline; high in ash; needs no added nitrogen.
• Steer manure: may be very high in salt; high in ash; needs no nitrogen; may have a strong odor.
• Compost: variable depending on what you put in it; must be well rotted, screened; needs no added nitrogen.

Sod — For an Instant Lawn

Here is some landscaping magic! You can convert your bare soil into sparkling turf in just a few hours—with sod. Sodding is essentially the transplanting of living grass with some roots attached.

Sod is more expensive than seed or stolons, but after the cost there is really no comparison. Buying seed or stolons is just the beginning. After the grass is in the ground, you have to rake it, mulch it, roll it, water it once or several times a day for 2 or 3 weeks; then you have to watch for seedling diseases, weeds, washouts, bird and animal damages, and other hazards. With sod, all you have to do is water thoroughly after the installation, stay off the lawn until it is rooted (from 10 days to 2 weeks), then just treat it like a mature lawn.

In addition to the savings in labor, there are some other advantages:
• A sodded lawn immediately covers up the mud or dust so it can't be tracked indoors.
• The sod is uniform, clean, and healthy when you install it. It has been treated to eliminate or prevent weeds, diseases, and insect pests.
• Sod is the most satisfactory way to establish a lawn under trees. It comes with its own roots so the grass does not have to compete with tree roots. Some seeded lawns never establish satisfactorily under trees because the tree roots continually edge out the young grass roots in the search for nutrients and water.

To install a sod lawn, the seedbed must first be properly prepared; instructions for soil preparation are given on pages 8–9. The finished grade before installing sod should be 1–1½ inches below the surrounding surfaces. The turf farm where you purchase the sod may recommend adding fertilizer before the sod is rolled out; the farm normally will provide the correct fertilizer.

Unroll the sod on the prepared soil (see illustration, right). Lay the strips parallel, with the strip ends staggered as in the bricklayers' running bond pattern. Press each successively laid strip snugly up against the one next to it. At the corners and edges, and around sidewalks, trim away any excess sod with a sharp knife.

Feel the joints after laying each strip.

If one side is low or high, fill in with loose soil under the low side or remove some of the excess soil under the high side. The only way to level uneven joints is with the final rolling, but that is effective only if the soil beneath is moist or soft.

After all the sod is laid out, roll the entire lawn with a roller half filled with water to smooth out any rough spots and to bond the sod to the soil.

Now, all you have to do is water a little more carefully than usual for a few days. Aside from that, it's as if the lawn has been yours for years. You won't have early weeding because there will be no bare soil for weeds to germinate and grow in.

To find turf farms, check with your local nursery or garden center or look in the Yellow Pages of your telephone directory under "Sod & Sodding Service." Depending on the supplier and your climate, you can choose from many kinds of turf: fine-bladed hardy grasses, blends, Bermuda grasses, dichondra, and some other local specialties.

For instructions on how to seed a lawn, see pages 8–9. If you want to use stolons or sprigs, see page 31. To plant by plugging from flats, see page 37.

Unroll sod strips in parallel rows with ends staggered as illustrated. Seams between strips should be tight and level—be careful not to overlap edges. Sod strips usually come from 15 to 18 inches wide, 4 or 5 feet long.

Trim away excess sod with sharp knife at corners, edges, along walks. Be sure cut edges fit snugly.

Roll entire yard with half-filled roller when all sod is unrolled, trimmed; evens out lumpy seams.

Seeding a Lawn

Whether you're putting in a first lawn at a new house or replacing old, weedy, patchy turf, the extra time and effort you spend in site preparation and proper seeding will save you from dealing with a troublesome lawn later. The step-by-step method of lawn installation shown here will get your lawn off to a good start.

If you're replanting an old lawn, your first step will be to strip off the old sod. It's better to remove the sod completely, rather than till it into the soil where the clumps could take years to decompose and may interfere with proper water drainage and new root development. You can remove the old grass layer with a rented power sod cutter (Step 1); or you can use a sharp, flat-backed, square-ended spade. Haul the old sod to a dump.

Once the sod is stripped off, use a rotary tiller to till the soil from 6 to 9 inches deep (Step 2). If your soil is especially hard and dry, soak it to a depth of 12 inches, then let it dry until it's workable. Soil can be tilled when it's crumbly and easy to work with a spade. Don't till muddy soil.

Spread a layer of soil amendments on the soil (Step 3), then till them in thoroughly. Level the tilled soil with a rented two-wheeled leveler or use a board scraper (Step 4). Leveling helps eliminate any unwanted hills and gulleys. At the same time, you should also create adequate drainage. Build up or slope the surface so that excess water will flow off and not puddle.

If you plan to install a sprinkler system, do it at this point. (See pages 14–15 for a step-by-step sprinkler system installation.) Then use a roller one third full of water to finish the leveling and contouring (Step 5).

Sow the grass seed evenly, either by handcasting (Step 6) or with a fertilizer spreader, following the package directions exactly. Rake the area to cover the seeds lightly and scatter them evenly (Step 7). Then cover the seeds with a thin layer of peat moss or other organic mulch (Step 8). If you use peat moss, be sure to moisten it well before you spread it or it won't absorb water later.

Next, apply a lawn fertilizer evenly over the new lawn with a mechanical spreader, following the directions on the fertilizer bag. Don't use a fertilizer combined with a weed killer or weed preventer. For further information on fertilizing, see pages 16–17.

Water the newly seeded lawn with a sprinkler or hose nozzle adjusted to deliver a gentle rain. Moisten the soil about 4 to 6 inches down, but don't allow the water to puddle or wash seed and soil away. Water again whenever the top of the soil looks dry—two or three times a day is about right.

The final step is to erect a barrier to keep people and dogs from walking over the newly seeded area. You can remove the barrier in about two months, after you've mowed the lawn a few times.

You can rent any of the equipment mentioned at your local garden center or garden equipment supply store; you are usually charged a daily rate for it.

Need to Control Weeds?

If weeds present a real problem in your area, you can mix calcium cyanamide into the soil with the soil amendments at Step 3. Calcium cyanamide will kill any weed seeds present and supply nitrogen to the area, but you'll have to wait at least 30 days before sowing grass seeds. To follow this procedure, complete steps 1 through 3, adding the calcium cyanamide with the amendments; then complete Step 4.

After 30 days have passed, sow some radish seeds (they sprout quickly) to make sure the calcium cyanamide has worn off. When the radishes sprout, the soil is safe again. Finish the leveling and contouring with a light roller (Step 5), seed the lawn, and add a fertilizer containing only phosphorus and potassium.

Soil Levelers You Can Make

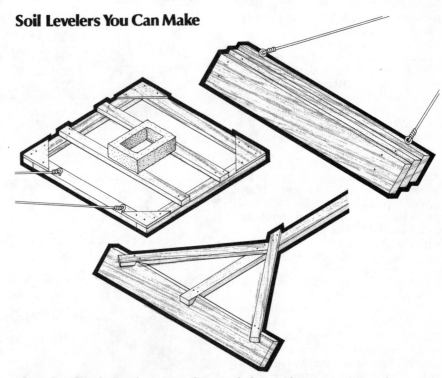

Three handmade levelers: (top) drag made by overlapping a series of planks so drag rides on down-facing edges; (center) window-frame drag— four planks in a square with a weight on top; (lower) straight-edge of 1x6 board forms a T with 2x2 handle.

Eight Steps to a New Lawn

Step 1: Remove sod layer with power sod cutter.

Step 2: Till soil from 6 to 9 inches deep with a rotary tiller.

Step 3: Spread a layer of soil amendment on soil; mix it in thoroughly.

Step 4: Level tilled soil.

Step 5: Finish leveling, contouring with roller ⅓ full of water.

Step 6: Sow grass seed by hand or with a spreader.

Step 7: Rake seeded area to lightly cover seeds.

Step 8: Cover seeds with a thin layer of mulch.

Lawn Watering—Here's How

A lush green lawn depends on an efficient watering system. Gardeners who live in areas that receive frequent summer rains will only need to supplement the natural moisture during occasional dry spells, but those who live in hot dry climates or areas that seldom receive summer rains will need to water on a regular basis. In either case, an understanding of how water, soil, and plant roots interact will be helpful.

Perhaps the most common question asked by gardeners is "How often should I water my lawn?" The answer depends on several factors: your soil type; the type of grass you have and how deep its root system can go; your climate; the season; and how you apply the water. The best rule of thumb for lawn watering is this: water thoroughly and infrequently.

How Soils and Water Interact

When you apply water to soil, the water moves down through the soil by progressively wetting soil particles. Each soil particle acquires a film of water; then any additional drops move down to wet lower particles. Water always moves downward, with very little lateral movement except on the surface.

The amount of water a particular soil can hold is called its holding capacity or field capacity. Only when the topsoil layer has acquired its holding capacity can remaining water move down to the next soil layer.

Field capacity varies according to soil type; each type retains a certain amount of water before allowing the rest to sink deeper. Clay soils have many fine particles and can hold more water than sandy soils, which have fewer, coarser particles. Field capacity for loamy soils falls somewhere in between that of clay and sandy soils.

Because of the difference in holding capacity, you will need to add more water to clay than to sandy soil to moisten the lower soil layers. It will take more time, but clay soils need water less often.

How to Water Thoroughly

A little water wets only a little soil. You can't dampen soil to any depth by watering it lightly. You can have damp soil only by wetting it thoroughly, then letting it partially dry.

Plant roots develop and grow in the presence of water, air, and nutrients, and most grasses will send roots down into all the soil layers that contain these essentials. If you keep only the top few inches of soil moist, the root system will remain shallow—and turf with shallow roots can be severely damaged in a sudden hot spell since the roots can't go deeper in search of water.

If you water deeply, roots will be encouraged to grow deeper and can search out moisture in lower soil layers. This chart, prepared by the University of California, shows how deep various grasses can send their roots:

Cool-season grasses	Root depth
Annual bluegrass	1 to 4 inches
Creeping bentgrass	4 to 18 inches
Colonial bentgrass	9 to 18 inches
Kentucky bluegrass	9 to 30 inches
Red fescue	9 to 30 inches
Tall fescue	18 to 48 inches

Warm-season grasses	
St. Augustine	1½ to 6 feet
Zoysia	1½ to 6 feet
Bermuda	1½ to 8 feet

Lawns can be kept green with daily light sprinklings, but this practice produces shallow root systems and necessitates continued daily light waterings during the growing season. If you water deeply, grass roots will extend deeper into the soil; you will have to apply more water with each sprinkling to moisten the lower soil layers, but you can water less frequently since the soil will lose moisture more slowly.

How Climate Affects Watering

If temperature, humidity levels, wind, and day length never varied, you could water according to a calendar. But climates do differ and so must watering. Plants need more water during their growing season than when they're dormant. They also need more water during hot or windy weather since heat and wind cause rapid evaporation. Conversely, plants need less water on cool or humid days when moisture loss is reduced.

One watering rule that can be applied to all types of soils and climates is this: test the soil. If the top 3 to 4 inches are dry, especially if it's the growing season, you probably need to water. The best way to test the soil is to plunge something long, such as a trowel, a spade, or a sharp stick, into the lawn to see how far down the wetness goes—ease of entry means the soil is adequately moist.

Using Sprinklers Effectively

The simplest way to apply water over a large expanse of turf is by sprinkling: sprinkling produces artificial rainfall. When you use a sprinkler, you can easily compute the amount of water to apply and determine how long it will take your sprinkler to deliver it.

An inch of water will penetrate 12 inches in sandy soil, about 7 inches in loamy soil, and from 4 to 5 inches in clay. If your grass has roots 12 inches deep, you'll need to apply 1

Depth in inches from bottom of furrow

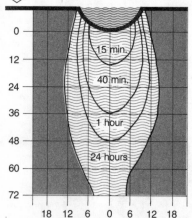

Water moves downward in soil with little lateral movement.

Soil Types and Water Penetration

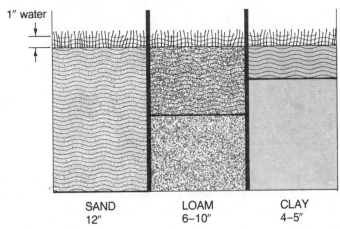

1" water

| SAND | LOAM | CLAY |
| 12" | 6–10" | 4–5" |

Water is slower in penetrating clay soils than sand or loam.

inch of water in sandy soil, about 2 inches in loam, and about 2½ to 3 inches in clay.

Next, you need to determine how much "rain" your sprinklers produce. Place several coffee cans at regular intervals in a direct line extending out from the sprinkler head. Then turn on the water to find out how long it takes to fill the containers to 1 inch. This will also help you determine how even the sprinkler pattern is (some containers will fill faster than others). When you know how long it takes your sprinkler to emit an inch of water, just multiply this time interval by the number of inches you need to supply. Sprinkler types and patterns are discussed on page 13.

Some Watering Tips

The following pointers may help you solve any watering problems you might encounter:

● The best time to water your lawn is early morning or late at night when there's no wind and when water pressure will be high.

● If you live in an arid climate where water shortages could occur, but you still want a lawn, consider planting more drought-tolerant grasses. If you live in a cool-season area, try tall fescue varieties. In a warm-season area, plant Bermuda grasses, St. Augustine grass, Zoysia grasses, Bahia grass, or Centipede grass. Bermudas are the most drought-tolerant grasses because of their very deep roots.

● If you have a water runoff problem due to heavy clay soil or dry subsoil, you can have the lawn aerated with an aerator that removes plugs of soil. (Spiking soil isn't recommended because the spikes are likely to compact the soil around the holes they drive.)

Other solutions to runoff problems include slowing down the delivery rate of your sprinkler so the soil can absorb the water, or selecting a sprinkler that emits water more slowly. Another good solution is to run sprinklers at full rate until runoff starts, shut them off for a half-hour so the soil can absorb the water, then repeat the process.

● An observant turf gardener may be able to judge when a lawn needs water by its appearance. Grass shows its need for water first by loss of resilience. When you walk across it, the grass doesn't spring back. Next, the color changes from fresh green and takes on a dull, gray green overcast. Then grass tops turn brown and die.

Once you can sense this timing, try to water just before the loss of resilience. Don't let your lawn get to the brown stage; it will take considerable time to come back from the crowns.

How to Check Your Sprinkler's Water Dispersion

Test "rainfall" from sprinkler by spacing coffee cans at varying distances and measuring output.

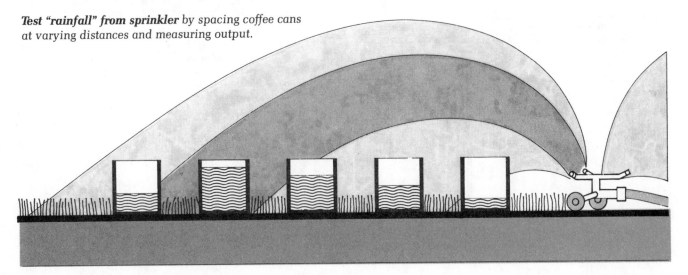

Choosing a Garden Hose

Garden hoses come in different lengths, colors, materials, and most important to your watering, different diameters. Regardless of your water pressure, the amount of water you get through a hose is in direct proportion to the hose's inside diameter. The illustrations shown below compare the water output delivered by three different hose diameters—a ½-inch, a ⅝-inch, and a ¾-inch-diameter hose—in a 15-second interval.

Standard hose sizes for home garden use are ½, ⅝, and ¾-inch diameter. The smallest diameter commonly sold, ⁷⁄₁₆ inch, is too small to be recommended for general gardening. You may also come across a 1-inch-diameter hose, but most gardeners find it difficult to use.

When you buy a hose, avoid the super-bargains. They seldom last very long and may be quite troublesome. The best indication of a good hose is a guarantee. Don't buy one without guarantee or warranty—it's that simple.

Two other factors to consider in choosing a hose are its weight and storage size. The ¾-inch hose weighs about twice as much as the ½-inch hose—both empty and full of water—and will take more effort to move around. You'll also have to provide twice as much storage space for the ¾-inch hose.

What Size Garden Hose?

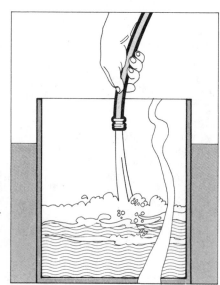

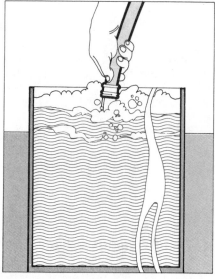

A ½-inch-diameter hose fills a 5-gallon jar about ⅓ full in 15 seconds. Hose is lightweight, easy to store. Best for small jobs, minimal planting.

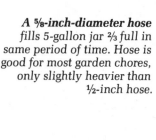

A ⅝-inch-diameter hose fills 5-gallon jar ⅔ full in same period of time. Hose is good for most garden chores, only slightly heavier than ½-inch hose.

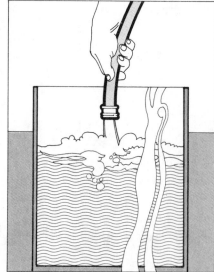

A ¾-inch-diameter hose fills 5-gallon jar in 15 seconds; it can put an inch of water on a 1,500-square-foot lawn in 39 minutes with pressure of 50 pounds per square inch. Hose is very heavy, hard to store. Some sprinklers may require this diameter hose.

Sprinklers — What to Look for

When you look for a sprinkler, the myriad types available in garden centers can be mind-boggling. To make your decision easier, we have grouped the various types of sprinklers according to the kind of watering pattern they produce.

Most sprinklers fall into one of five watering patterns. These five patterns are illustrated on this page, along with pertinent information to help you decide which sprinkler will do the best job in your garden. To be effective, almost all the sprinklers' watering patterns require some overlapping of use.

Sprinkler Units

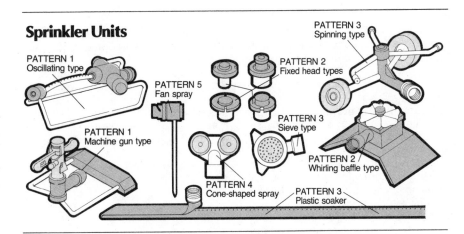

PATTERN 1
Oscillating type

PATTERN 1
Machine gun type

PATTERN 5
Fan spray

PATTERN 3
Spinning type

PATTERN 2
Fixed head types

PATTERN 3
Sieve type

PATTERN 2
Whirling baffle type

PATTERN 4
Cone-shaped spray

PATTERN 3
Plastic soaker

Sprinkler Patterns

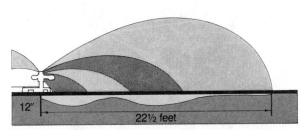

12"   22½ feet

Pattern 1 is effective if you move sprinkler to overlap. Oscillating type and rotating "machine gun" type sprinklers make this pattern.

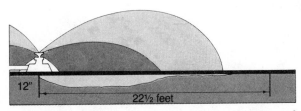

12"   22½ feet

Pattern 2 has most water dropping on inside; you need successive overlaps. Whirling baffle type and fixed heads work this way.

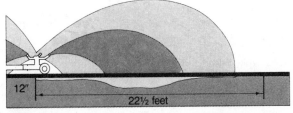

12"   22½ feet

Pattern 3 is useful but erratic; most water falls 4 to 8 feet out. Plastic soakers, types with revolving arms, sieve types deliver water this way.

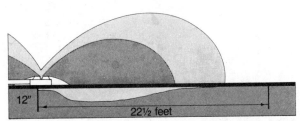

12"   22½ feet

Pattern 4 cone spray soaks only a small area; for best results, turn water to half-pressure, move sprinkler often. One cone spray has two big holes like owl's eyes.

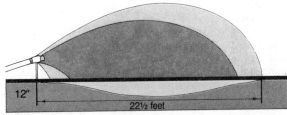

12"   22½ feet

Pattern 5 fan spray throws most of water 7 to 14 feet from sprinkler. Nailhead spike type sprays water through slit in its head.

Installing a Sprinkler System

If you live in a climate where lawn watering is a regular garden chore, you may want to consider installing a sprinkler system. The ideal time to put in a system is when you are planting a new lawn or reseeding an old one (for further information on timing, see pages 8–9). You can install sprinklers in existing lawns, but the job requires trenching, laying the pipes, backfilling, then seeding or sodding the trench scars. If you remove sod carefully when you dig the trench, you can recycle it.

Putting in your own system isn't difficult if you use the solvent-welded PVC (polyvinyl chloride) piping. For tools, you'll need a shovel or spade, a pipe wrench, a hacksaw, a file or sharp knife, a tape measure, and a soil tamper.

You can start by contacting sprinkler system companies for help in working out a master plan (look in the Yellow Pages under "Sprinklers—Garden & Lawn Parts & Supplies," "Irrigation Systems & Equipment," or "Landscape Equipment & Supplies"). The company you contact will need some information from you: the size of your lawn, the type of grass you plan to use, locations of permanent plantings and structures such as buildings or fences, and the location of your water source. A scale map of your garden and outdoor plumbing will also be helpful.

The company will also need to know the diameter of the water supply pipe and whether it's made of galvanized iron or copper, your water pressure (most sprinkler system companies will lend or rent you a pressure gauge), and the size of your water meter (check with your water company for this information).

The company that sells you the parts for your system will provide assembly instructions. The seven steps illustrated on these pages give you a general picture of the procedure to follow in a typical lawn installation. Here are some additional hints that may make your job easier:

• First, you may find it helpful to attach an extra valve to shut off water to the sprinklers while you install them without turning off your whole water system. (An illustration of this extra valve is shown at upper right in Step 2 on the horizontal pipe that holds the faucet.)

• Put the system together one piece at a time. PVC pipe comes in 10-foot sections. As you need shorter lengths, measure carefully and cut pieces with a hacksaw, keeping the cut as square as possible. Remove burrs with file or sharp knife.

• When you weld parts together, you must work quickly. The plastic solvent adheres quite rapidly—and once the pipe's welded, joints cannot be broken apart. You may find it helpful to practice a few welds before you start. To weld, daub plastic solvent on both pipe pieces, connect them tightly, and give them a half twist to make a good seal.

• After installing the control valve on the first section of pipe (Step 2), let the welds dry at least 6 hours, then test the pipe for leaks; this section

Step 1: Dig 8-inch-deep trenches for pipes. String tied to stakes helps you keep trench straight.

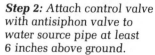

Step 2: Attach control valve with antisiphon valve to water source pipe at least 6 inches above ground.

Step 3: Assemble pipe with sprinkler head, riser already fitted onto end. Keep riser upright when joining.

will always remain under constant pressure.

Automate Your Sprinklers

Lawn watering can be made effortless by placing your system on a timer. Sprinkler supply companies carry a variety of timers and can help you in choosing the best one for your particular system.

An automated sprinkler system can also make your lawn watering more efficient. Set your timer to activate the sprinklers late at night or very early in the morning when it's windless and cool and water pressure is at its highest level.

Plastic Pipes and Pipe Fittings

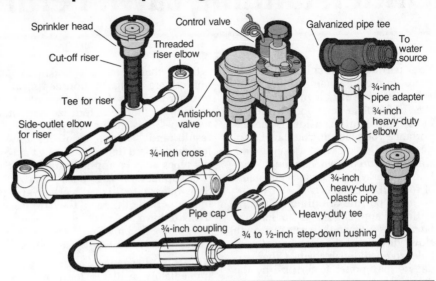

Sprinkler head
Control valve
Galvanized pipe tee
To water source
Cut-off riser
Threaded riser elbow
¾-inch pipe adapter
Tee for riser
Antisiphon valve
¾-inch heavy-duty elbow
Side-outlet elbow for riser
¾-inch cross
¾-inch heavy-duty plastic pipe
Pipe cap
Heavy-duty tee
¾-inch coupling
¾ to ½-inch step-down bushing

Step 4: Continue assembling system from water source outward. Overhead view shows branches running from central cross.

Step 6: Fill in trenches, mounding loose soil above ground level along center of trench.

Step 5: Test for leaks, proper coverage after welds are dry and after first flushing out pipes with sprinkler heads removed. Repair leaks before burying pipes.

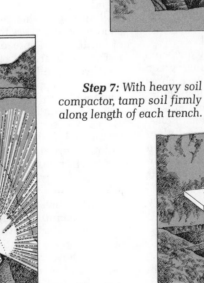

Step 7: With heavy soil compactor, tamp soil firmly along length of each trench.

Understanding Lawn Fertilizers

Your particular gardening habits will probably dictate when and how often you fertilize your lawn and which type of fertilizer you choose. Another factor you should consider is the importance you place on your lawn's appearance. Do you want a deep green, well-manicured lawn, or a rough-and-tumble grassy surface for a good game of football or croquet?

One good rule of thumb for timing fertilizer applications is to fertilize lawn grasses when their rate of growth slows down and the deep green color fades to a yellowish shade. Other gardeners may prefer to fertilize by the calendar—once a month during the growing season. Take a good look at the wide range of fertilizer products available and their diverse methods of treatment and application; you should find a product that will meet your particular gardening habits and your lawn's needs.

Choosing a Lawn Fertilizer

Providing sufficient nitrogen on a regular basis is the key to healthy looking grass. Whatever the product, the package label should contain three numbers, such as 26-3-3, 6-4-2, or 10-10-0. The first number is the most important; it refers to the percentage of nitrogen present. The second number refers to phosphorus, the third to potassium. If one of the numbers is zero, that element isn't included.

Nitrogen stimulates leaf growth and helps grass maintain a rich green color. Less important to lawns, phosphorus promotes sturdy cell structure and healthy root growth and aids in flower and fruit production. Potassium helps plants with normal plant functions and development. When you buy a fertilizer specifically formulated for grass, these three elements should be in proper balance.

Some fertilizer products also include herbicides or insecticides.

Nitrogen—Key to Green Lawns

Lawn fertilizers contain nitrogen in either an organic or inorganic form. Organic fertilizers work slowly because bacteria must convert them into nitrates that roots can assimilate. Sources are sludge, cottonseed meal, or other products derived from plants or animals. Inorganic fertilizers are of two types: "fast acting" for immediate results and "slow release" for prolonged nutrient delivery. The fast-acting types must be applied carefully as over-application will "burn" a lawn. Slow-release fertilizers work over a longer period of time so they are less likely to burn.

You may find nitrogen listed on fertilizer labels under these names:

Nitrate or nitrogenous. Nitrogen is an immediately available form; not dependent on air or soil temperatures. Fast-acting.

Ammoniacal or ammonic. Bacteria in soil are needed to break down the ammonia into nitrates. Fast-acting.

Urea. A more complex compound than ammonia; bacteria convert it to ammonia, then nitrates. Fast-acting; use with care to prevent burning.

Urea-form, urea-formaldehyde, or "slow-release." Artificially combined with resin to give slow, long-term release of usable nitrates.

How to Apply Fertilizers

On the next page, three of the most popular fertilizer spreading methods are illustrated. Whichever method you choose, be sure to use the right amount of fertilizer and spread it evenly.

The fertilizer package label should give you guidelines for the best method of application, the correct amount of fertilizer to apply and any other procedures you should follow. Most labels state that fertilizers must be watered in thoroughly after application to avoid burning the grasses. For the best results, follow these directions exactly.

The University of California Agricultural Extension recommends applying 1 pound of actual nitrogen per 1,000 square feet of lawn once a month during periods of active growth. To find out how many pounds of nitrogen your bag of fertilizer contains, check the first number (the nitrogen symbol) on the three-number formula; it gives the percentage of the actual amount of nitrogen your bag contains. If you have a 10-pound bag of 10-10-0 fertilizer, the nitrogen content is 10 percent of 10 pounds, or 1 pound of actual nitrogen. This does not apply to "slow-release" fertilizers.

Whichever fertilizer applicator you choose, be sure to clean it thoroughly after each use. Don't wash a metal hopper unless you plan to dry and oil it. To let out excess fertilizer, just spin the wheel and tap the hopper's sides, or wipe it out with a clean cloth.

By hand. You can use this method of applying fertilizer with any type of solid fertilizer, but it's safest with organic fertilizers since the danger of grass burn is less. Handcast the fertilizer across the lawn in one direction, applying at full strength. Then repeat at right angles using only half as much. If you think you've applied too much fertilizer in certain spots, rake the area lightly to spread it out more evenly.

Spraying liquid fertilizers. A hose-end proportioner is a good way to apply liquid fertilizers if you work quickly and carefully. Divide the lawn in half with a rope or sticks; spray evenly, trying to reach the halfway point when the proportioner is half full, then finish the rest of the lawn as it empties.

Using applicators. Two types of fertilizer applicators are commonly used: a crank-operated broadcaster and a wheeled hopper. The crank-operated broadcaster works well for pelletized fertilizer. Use the wheeled hopper for any dry fertilizer.

The crank-operated broadcaster throws fertilizer pellets over a 20-foot diameter. Use your left hand to operate the rate-of-flow lever. Start at one end of your lawn, make a run, pace off the swath diameter, then begin your next parallel run. Since this broadcasts in a complete circle, plan on having the front of you thoroughly covered with fertilizer.

Although you can rent wheeled hoppers, it's best to purchase your own so you know it's clean and in good working order. You'll use the open-and-shut lever often. You spread a strip of fertilizer, close the opening, reposition the hopper, then spread the next strip, putting the hopper in motion before reopening the lever.

Broadcasting by hand or applicator
Handcast fertilizer (far left) by walking slowly, casting parallel strips, then crossing the area at right angles for even coverage. To use a hand-crank centrifugal feeder (left), turn handle at even rate and walk in parallel strips. Hand-crank feeder can throw pelletized fertilizer over a 20-foot diameter.

Liquid feeding
Fill hose-end proportioner with correct amount of fertilizer, water (left). Mark halfway point on lawn, proportioner. Walk evenly, start spraying. Halfway point (center) should be reached when jar is half empty. Continue to end (right), moving proportioner up and down to spread spray evenly.

Hopper feeding
Start with two strips at each end of lawn (left) to give you turning room. You want an even pattern with no overlaps or uncovered strips. To get this, shut off hopper just as you reach end strips; turn and start moving before you reopen hopper. Hopper wheel (right) should roll just inside previous strip. Shut off hopper (center) at end strips or you'll leave a double dose.

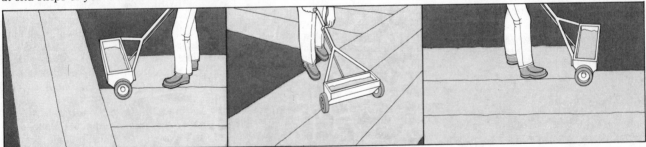

Avoid these hopper mistakes
Running hopper like a lawn mower will result in uncovered areas at every turn. These spots show up later as yellow or pale marks.

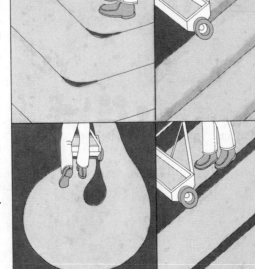

Hairpin turns leave tear-drop-shaped areas that will become yellow or pale as fertilized grass turns green.

Uneven walking or stopping and starting with the hopper open can cause a double dose of fertilizer, which may burn grass in rectangular patches or cause uneven growth.

Unless you set one hopper wheel just inside previous track, full-length strips of lawn will not be fertilized.

Good Maintenance—a Must

Different grasses require different up-keep, and different homeowners have different ideas about what a well-groomed lawn should look like. But, most people will agree that lawns need to be mowed, trimmed or edged, and occasionally weeded to keep them looking their best.

In this section, we look at the various types of lawn mowers available, discuss the proper techniques of mowing, and deal with trimming, edging, and weeding. The more specialized maintenance jobs of de-thatching and aerating are discussed on page 32.

Mowing and Mowers

Two basic types of mowers are available—the reel mower (either power or hand-operated) and the rotary mower. Both types offer certain advantages as well as some possible drawbacks. You should look at the various points made about each type, then look at your particular lawn situation to determine which mower is best for you.

The Reel-mowing Principle

Any reel mower, hand or power-driven, makes a comparatively smooth and even cut. You get neat little cross-wise marks and a "striped" effect on the overall lawn. (Loose reel bearings or dull blades may emphasize this effect.)

The typical reel mower has five blades, although some models may have only four blades or as many as six or seven (those models with six or seven blades are for cutting low or wiry grass, such as Bermuda and bent which thrive on very close mowing). All reel mowers cut only when moving in the forward direction.

With a reel mower that has no grass catcher, mow in a counterclockwise direction if your mower throws to the left, clockwise if it throws to the right (all reel mowers throw their cuttings out in one direction, depending on which way the blades spiral or twist). That way the mower will deposit part of the clippings on uncut

grass. Then on the next parallel trip, the mower will chop up some of the previous run's clippings—an advantage because finely cut clippings sift down into grass better than longer pieces.

If your mower leaves rough spots on the lawn surface or if tough blades of grass pass through the blades un-scathed, the blades are probably dull or out of alignment, or both, and the mower should be serviced.

The hand-operated reel mower. If you like exercise and you feel your garden should be a place of peace and quiet, the hand-operated machine may be for you. With a small lawn (2,000 square feet or less), time isn't a significant factor, but in terms of physical energy, your legs and back must take the place of the power-driven mower.

Hand-operated reel mowers are less expensive than power mowers, are easy to store, and require a minimum of maintenance. To keep a hand mower at its best, keep the bearings oiled with a light household oil (if it's for lawn mowers, the label will say so) and have the blades sharpened annually.

The power reel mower. Two features make the power reel mower especially suitable for hilly lawns: it fits into the contours easily and its power-driven wheels take it up slopes and hold it on course. Most power reel mowers are self-propelled; the engine drives both the blades and the wheels.

Power reel mowers generally cost slightly more than power rotary mowers and are considered to be somewhat safer, although this is relative—no machine with power-drive and fast-moving sharp blades is really safe.

The power reel mower is for use on lawns only. For cutting high grass and tall weeds, chopping leaves and other debris, and operating on rough ground, a gasoline-powered rotary mower is much more efficient.

The Power Rotary Mower

Unlike the reel mower, which uses a scissor action, a rotary mower cuts like a scythe or a knife. There are several types of rotary blades, having

sickle bar sections or freely pivoting blades mounted at the end of the large blade or at the edge of one or two horizontal discs. The sickle bar sections and freely pivoting blades are easy to sharpen or replace.

All rotary mowers cut only with the outer edge of the rotating blade. Most are available with grass catching attachments.

Two outstanding advantages of the rotary mower are its ability to cut high weeds, stalks, and grass, and its ability to cut close to trees, walls, and other structures. Also, it effectively chops leaves on the lawn.

The rotary's cutting height differs from that of the reel. You can adjust the rotary higher, but not as low. Unlike reel mowers, the rotary mower cuts in either direction. This makes it easier to handle, especially on small or oddly shaped lawn areas. Some rotary mowers have a flip-over handle so you can make the return trip without turning the machine around.

A well-made, large, gasoline-powered rotary mower is usually tougher than the typical reel mower or an electric-powered rotary. It can take rough treatment that would normally damage a reel. Rotary blades can hit rocks and sticks and knock them out without killing the engine. Resultant nicks or cuts on the blades can be filed down, or if the blades look too hopeless, just replace them. Note: Never try to file a reel mower's blades yourself—the job requires special equipment, so take it to a professional.

A sharp rotary blade makes a clean cut and requires less power to operate than a dull one. Dull blades mash the grass tips, leaving a brownish cast on the cut surface.

Electric or Gasoline Power?

Most power mowers sold are gasoline driven, but you can buy an electric rotary mower if you choose to.

The advantages and shortcomings of the electric machine are briefly stated. An electric machine is limited by the total length of its cord and the power and speed of the motor. Usually, you must cut the lawn in a back and forth pattern, gradually working away from the outdoor electric outlet to keep from snarling or cutting the cord. If you lawn is very large, electric outlets are far away, or you have several trees to dodge, an electric mower may just be too much trouble. Use of extension cords is not encouraged, but if you do use one, be sure it is a heavy-duty grounded one.

The motors on most electric mowers turn more slowly than gasoline-powered motors. This means you can't use an electric mower for heavy-duty, tall weed cutting.

On the plus side, an electric mower is quiet, easy to start, and completely without fumes. On small lawns it does the job quickly and easily.

Buying a Mower

When you shop for a power mower, let your dealer know what you need it for. Tell him or her how large your lawn is, what type grass you have, if you have a hilly lawn, or if you expect to cut tall weeds.

It's best to have the dealer demonstrate the mower for you and explain the maintenance requirements. If you plan to store your mower over the winter months, ask if any special care is needed.

How Frequently Should You Mow?

Some experts recommend mowing so frequently that you never remove more than ⅓ of the total grass blade surface. The theory is that cutting off a greater portion can cause a physiological shock to the plant because production of food is curtailed.

In practice, many gardeners find it hard to avoid cutting off more than ⅓ of the blade—especially if the lawn has been fertilized within the past few weeks and the person who does the mowing has time to do it only once a week.

If you must cut off more than ⅓ of the grass blade, don't worry about it, but do avoid making a habit of it. And when your grass has a growing spurt, try to mow more frequently.

Mowing Techniques

The height you should cut your lawn depends on the type of grass you are growing and your climate. Proper mowing heights for both cool-season and subtropical grasses are given on pages 28 and 31.

After mowing your lawn, check the cutting height (measure from the soil to the top of the grass blades) and make any necessary adjustment for future mowings. Don't rely on the mower measurements; they can't accurately account for the distance the mower's wheels settle into the grass.

Mow at least weekly. Longer intervals between mowings result in too much grass being cut off. You can let short clippings stay on the lawn; they serve as a natural mulch and return some nutrients to the soil.

It's best not to mow wet grass: it will mash under the mower wheels, stick to the cutting blades, or just lie down under the mower and spring back later. If you must mow it, you can get rid of some surface moisture by brushing the grass with a piece of burlap or a tree branch.

If you rake up your grass clippings or use a grass catcher, don't let them accumulate in a pile—they're likely to become a breeding place for flies. The most efficient ways to use grass clippings are to put them in a compost pile or use them in very thin layers as a mulch for flower beds.

Trimming and Edging

Trimming grass along sidewalks, house walls, trees, fences, or garden beds can be done by hand with grass shears or with a powered trimmer such as the string trimmer illustrated on this page. Long-handled grass shears are back savers if you have a lot of edges to trim.

For a neat edge along walks, you can get a hand-operated edger with a rotating wheel that pulls grass across an upright cutting edge. This device needs a hard surface on the outside of the lawn edge to support the rubber drive wheel and give traction to turn the cutting wheel.

Weeding

Weeds spoil the smooth, even texture of a well-groomed lawn. You can attack them two ways: either with chemical controls (see pages 20–22 for weed-killing chemicals) or by hand pulling.

If you have only a few weeds, hand pulling or using a tool is the best method of attack. The notch-ended weeder shown below works perfectly in the tight quarters between grass plants. Try to remove as much of the weed's root as possible.

The trowel and cultivator are more useful for dealing with weeds at the lawn's edge or near ground covers.

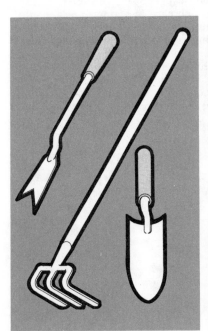

Weeding tools include a notch-ended weeder (left); a cultivator, either long or short-handled (center); a trowel (right).

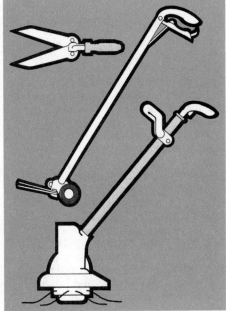

Trimming tools are hand-operated grass shears (top), long-handled grass shears with wheels for stand-up position (center), nylon string trimmer with a motor (lower).

Lawn Ailments

Not only do lawns provide a soft green mat to walk on, play on, lie on, or just admire, they also provide an excellent breeding ground for unsightly weeds, militant insects, and grass-destroying diseases. Grassy carpets can become battlefields where we combat one or all of these lawn-destroying elements.

Infrequently, the cause of our sickly looking lawn cannot be blamed on weeds, pests, or diseases. Rather, it's the result of a physical or mechanical ailment, such as deep shade or soil compaction. These problems are discussed on page 24.

Weeds—The Lawn Spoilers

Technically, weeds are annual or perennial plants growing where they are unwanted. As long as soil provides the necessary environment for plants to grow, weeds will grow too. Most soils already contain dormant weed seeds which only need the right germinating conditions to sprout.

You may wonder why last year's weed-free lawn has weeds in it this year. Where do the weed seeds come from? First, lawn seed is never 100 percent pure; all lawn seed comes contaminated with some weed seed. Gusty winds can disperse weed seeds for miles. And seed-dropping birds and foot traffic also aid in weed infestation.

Weeds are classified into two groups: broad-leafed weeds and grassy weeds. The weed chart on page 21 illustrates 15 of the most commonly found weeds.

The Broad-leafed Weeds

The term "broad-leafed weeds" describes all weeds that are not grass-like. Many of these broad-leafed weeds, like chickweed and spotted spurge, have leaves only the size of large freckles.

Grassy Weeds

Any grass that destroys the even texture and uniform color of a lawn is considered a weed grass. The list of these grassy weeds is long. Some of the most common grassy weeds are annual bluegrass, Bermuda grass, crabgrass, dallisgrass, quackgrass, and rye grass. With the exception of Bermuda grass and quackgrass, you can pull grassy weeds by hand or with a steel weed knife. To combat the more tenacious grassy weeds, you can choose from an assortment of chemical weed killers (see chart, page 21.)

Crabgrass—king of grassy weeds. True crabgrass is king of the grassy weeds. But gardeners everywhere often mistake other grassy weeds for crabgrass. This frequently results in the use of crabgrass-killing chemicals on weeds that won't be fazed by them. On the other hand, if your lawn really is infested by crabgrass, you should learn how to recognize it and how to get rid of it.

What is crabgrass? Hairy crabgrass (*Digitaria sanguinalis*) is a weedy annual that infests turf areas, lawns, and landscapes. Seeds germinate as early as February in warmer areas, continuing through summer. Small seedlings grow 2 to 4 leaves that finally form large, flat, stem-rooting, weedy clumps in summer. Mature, pale green blades grow 2–5 inches long and $\frac{1}{3}$ inch wide, with undersides covered in coarse tiny hairs. Fingerlike flower

Hairy crabgrass

spikelets arise from 2–6-inch-high narrow stems. The flowers seed heav-

ily, so immediate eradication of the weed is necessary to prevent a crabgrass infestation next year. To control, hand pull the crabgrass or use a specified crabgrass control.

Smooth crabgrass (*Digitaria ischaemum*) resembles hairy crabgrass, but grows smaller and is not as hairy.

Smooth crabgrass

Bermuda grass, a very deep-rooted and invasive grass, is groomed as a lawn in many of the warmer southern regions of the country where it thrives. But Bermuda grass is considered a weed in a cool-season grass lawn. Try pulling out isolated sprigs before roots establish a deep foothold. If the weed infestation gets ahead of you, spot treat the weeds with dalapon—one of the proven chemical controls for Bermuda grass.

Quackgrass flourishes in cool, moist, or dry climates and in almost any soil. It's a perennial that grows from scaly rhizomes. A rhizome is a thickened underground stem that spreads by creeping. With quackgrass, these rhizomes branch at almost every node, forming a dense root mass for which the plant is notorious and despised. Any small piece of rhizome left in the soil will grow a new plant. Do not let this grass go to seed, as the seeds are long lived and may lie dormant in the soil for as long as 2 to 4 years, then will suddenly sprout new plants. Leaves are dark green in most climates; in dry areas they are covered with a whitish bloom. The portion of

Note: The fifteen weeds shown below are commonly found in lawns. Under each weed name is listed the chemical or chemicals effective against that particular weed. Most of these weed killers are common chemical names, not brand names. Any weed killer you purchase should have the chemical name, the specific weeds it will control, and the types of grass you can apply it to listed on the label.

The Broad-leafed Weeds

Broad-leaf plantain
2, 4-D amine

Chickweed
MCPP, Dicamba

Clover
MCPP, Dicamba

Common dandelion
2, 4-D amine

Curly dock
Dicamba, 2, 4-D

English daisy
Dicamba

Knotweed
Dicamba

Red sorrel
Dicamba

Spurge
No effective chemical available

Yarrow
2, 4-D ester

The Grassy Weeds

Annual bluegrass
Bensulide

Bermuda grass
Dalapon

Dallisgrass
DSMA

Quackgrass
Dalapon (effective in dichondra only)

Rye grass
Dalapon

the leaf that sheaths the stem is often hairy. Hand pick quackgrass from lawns and dig rhizomes from the soil, or treat them with a specified chemical control. (Chemical controls are listed on page 21.)

Controlling Weeds

Compared to the old days when every lawn weed had to be removed by hand, prying tool, or steel weed knife, today chemical weed controls simplify the work. Of course, if weeds are scarce, hand pulling with a weeding tool is still a good way to eradicate weeds. For weeding tools and their uses, see page 19 in our lawn maintenance chapter.

Weed killers. Keep in mind that it's most important to choose the right chemical at the appropriate time, following label directions exactly. If you ignore any of these steps, you'll waste time and money, and perhaps some plants.

If you use a chemical that kills weeds as they germinate, don't expect it to work unless you cover every inch of soil. Do not spray selective weed killers in the wind—wait for the wind to stop, then apply the material.

If you use a weed killer that is absorbed by the leaves of weeds, do not apply more than the directions call for. Overdoses may burn the leaves and prevent proper movement of the chemical down to the root system.

The previous page shows 15 of the most common weeds found growing in lawns. Under each weed is listed the chemical or chemicals effective against that particular weed.

It is most important to note that the weed killers mentioned are common chemical names and not brand names. Any weed killer you purchase should have the chemical name, the specific weeds it will kill, and the types of grass you can apply it to listed on the label.

Whatever type of weed killer you decide to use, remember to explicitly follow the directions on the container label.

Weed Killer Applicators

Fortunately there are many ways to apply weed killers. You may use applicator wands designed for spot application of chemicals to individual weeds, or trigger-type squirting oil cans.

Hose-end applicators, available in several styles, can be attached to a garden hose for applying water soluble chemicals (these are illustrated on page 17 in the fertilizing chapter). Apply these chemicals at low water pressure so as not to wash all the weed killer off the leaves.

Pressure spray tanks and simple watering cans are excellent devices for applying weed killers. Unfortunately, once they have been filled with a weed killing chemical, they should not be used for any purpose other than weed eradicating.

Dry fertilizer spreaders, shown on page 17, provide an efficient means for applying dry or granular weed killers.

Pests—The Garden Intruders

Lawn-damaging pests fall into two main groups: those that feed on leaf blades and other *above-ground* lawn parts, and those that feed on roots and other *below-ground* parts of grass plants.

Above-ground Pests

Armyworms, cutworms, sod webworms (lawn moth larvae), skipper larvae, leafhoppers, dichondra flea beetle, frit fly larvae, Bermuda mite, slugs and snails, and chinch bugs (the latter in eastern states) feed above ground. To get rid of these you first water the lawn, then apply the right insecticide (see "Choosing the Right Insecticide," below). After this, leave the lawn alone for a few days to allow the insecticide to do its job.

Below-ground Insects

White grubs, billbug grubs, Japanese beetle grubs (mostly in eastern states), and mole crickets are below-ground lawn pests. To rid your lawn of these, apply the correct insecticide and then drench your lawn with water. The water will carry the insecticide down deep to the root zone of the lawn where the menacing insects live.

Choosing the Right Insecticide

Unfortunately, the best method to control lawn insect infestation is through the use of insecticides. Selecting the correct lawn insecticide is easy. Diazinon insecticide works on most turf insects above or below the ground. The following insecticides work on one or more of the lawn-damaging pests: diazinon, dursban,
kelthane, malathion, metaldahyde, or mesurol.

Insect Symptoms, Causes and Control

In the paragraphs below we describe the damage caused by leading lawn pests, and effective insecticides to use against them. Check with your local cooperative extension service to make sure that the insecticide you choose is still registered for home use in your state.

• **Irregularly shaped brown areas: armyworms or sod webworms.** Most lawns, no matter what their age, are susceptible to attack by armyworms or sod webworms. These worms feed on grass crowns and bases of blades. In warmer climates they can destroy whole lawns. To control these invading insects, treat them with diazinon spray or granules, or with dursban spray or granules.

• **Dead spots 1 or 2 inches in diameter, with grass chewed below the mowing level: cutworms.** This pest makes a hole about the thickness of a pencil, leading down into the roots.

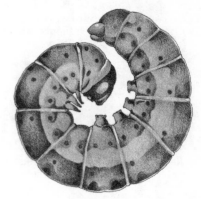

Cutworm

To control the chomping creatures, apply spray or granules of diazinon or dursban.

• **Orange, brown, and yellow butterflies fly over the lawn during the heat of the day: fiery skipper.** Symptoms other than butterflies are isolated round dead spots, 1–2 inches in diameter, eventually fusing and killing large areas of the lawn. Small brownish-yellow worms may be inside and underneath the patches of dead grass. Sometimes white cottony masses show in the lawn. These cottonlike masses are the cocoons of a parasite that preys on the larvae of the skipper. If this biological control is not apparent in your lawn, then apply diazinon in spray or granules.

The following test will tell you definitely whether your pest is just one or a combination of armyworms, sod webworms, cutworms, fiery skipper, or something else (the most likely other cause is brown patch, discussed later in this chapter).

Mix 1 teaspoon of liquid detergent Vel (University of California at Davis has tried other detergents, but for some reason Vel works best) in a sprinkling can of water. If gray worms or caterpillars wiggle to the surface within 10 minutes, your lawn is infested with any of the above. In matted bent grass, it may take longer for the webworms to appear.

• **Dead grass in defined patches: white grubs or billbug grubs.** Pull on the grass. If it comes up like a wet doormat, it's probably a victim of white grubs. You may even find some grubs underneath the grass that you pull— u-shaped grayish white worms (see illustration) shaped much like fat shrimp. If you are not squeamish, you can hand pick the worms and know that you've dealt with them in the most direct way. Replace the mat of brown grass. It may replenish itself from the roots in a few weeks.

For chemical control use diazinon or dursban for white grubs. After applying the chemical treatments, water the lawn heavily. This helps leach the chemicals into the ground where the larvae eat.

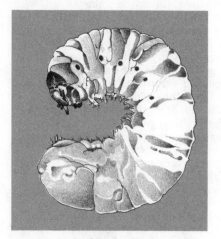

White grub

• **Central shoots of grass plants dead: frit fly.** The small black frit fly produces four generations of larvae a year. The spring and fall larvae live in young grass stems, eating and eventually killing the central shoots, causing the plant to send out side shoots. Some species of grass are very susceptible to this pest. Control the frit fly larvae with diazinon spray or kelthane.

• **Tufting and yellowing of Bermuda grass, accompanied by skin irritation when touched: Bermuda mite.** Spray with diazinon.

• **Grass seedlings uprooted, young grass blades severed from their roots: mole crickets.** These tiny creatures freeload in moist, light soils of newly seeded lawns. Burrowing into the ground, using their shovel-like front legs, they destroy seedlings as they excavate. To control mole crickets, spray with diazinon.

• **Slugs and snails on the grass at night.** Use mesurol or metaldehyde, or metaldehyde plus sevin. Apply this snail bait in the evening to a sprinkled or damp lawn. The moisture on the grass brings the snails and slugs out and activates the bait.

• **To control leafhoppers,** apply diazinon or malathion spray; use dursban or malathion spray to check flea beetles in dichondra, and chinch bugs in St. Augustine lawns.

Gophers and Moles

The success of a campaign to rid your lawn and garden of these pests often depends more on perseverance than on the type of control you use. The three controls used most frequently are the trap, poison, and gas.

Gophers are slipshod excavators. Their mounds are irregular, often fan shaped, the hole located where the handle of the fan would be. The hole is usually plugged up, but is still discernible.

Moles throw up round, conical mounds composed of looose chunks of earth from their main runs. They force plugs of earth up to the surface, but they do not open the tunnel. The ridges you see in your lawn where soil has been raised are hunting paths, and they are seldom used more than once.

Traps. Traps have two outstanding advantages over poison or gas—you actually see the dead gopher or mole, and trapping is the safest method of control. The Macabee trap is considered the most successful for gophers. The lateral-jawed type is most effective for moles.

Poison bait. Though less reliable than trapping, poison bait is the control preferred by many people because it requires less digging. Also, you can cover large areas faster with bait than with trapping. Pieces of vegetable root or dried prunes dusted with pow-

dered strychnine are very effective in poisoning gophers. For moles, dried fruit, vegetables, and grain baits with thalium sulfate as the toxic agent have proved to be highly successful.

Gas. Under certain conditions (damp, tight soil; limited runway system), gas either destroys gophers and moles or causes them to move out. It is more expensive than bait. Gasses that have been used successfully on gophers and moles include calcium cyanide, methyl bromide, carbon monoxide, and carbon disulphide.

Lawn Diseases

Often a well-maintained, vigorously growing lawn, supposedly free of insects and other pests, will suddenly turn yellow in random spots and begin to die. If this seems to be the problem in your lawn, it probably has a fungus disease.

A fungus disease is composed of microscopic, threadlike plant life. Fungi cannot produce their own food, so they live off dead or living plant matter. Lawns and their clippings seem a delectable favorite of certain kinds of fungi.

Good Turf Management

Before you decide to apply a fungicide to remedy your yellow, browning lawn, learn to diagnose its trouble.

Professional turf managers first decide if the watering and feeding schedule has been adequate.

Lack of water makes grass turn limp, then dull or smoky green; ultimately it will die. Lack of nitrogen makes grass turn yellowish or pale green. It grows slowly and becomes thin. Lack of either or both of these two essentials can lay a lawn open to all kinds of secondary troubles, including an array of fungus diseases that can ultimately cause death to lawns.

Most of the diseases and physical troubles of lawns become apparent by persisting after the lawn has been adequately watered and fed with nitrogen.

When Lawns Look Sick

If your lawn has been watered and fertilized consistently, and still appears sick, then it's time to examine it for disease.

Rarely does a lawn fungus show the classic symptoms that make identification easy, allowing you to proceed with the specific fungicide cure.

Usually when you inspect a sick lawn and compare its symptoms with book descriptions of fungus diseases, you'll find that your lawn fungus could have all or none of several symptoms—"brown patch," "melting out," "grease spot," "fusarium patch," "red thread" or "snow mold"— because the symptoms overlap. (See our fungus disease identification and control chart on page 25.)

Preventing Disease

Lawn fungus is much easier to prevent than to cure. The best way to avoid fungus diseases is to plant the grass that is right for the particular climate and surroundings in which it must grow.

Next, care for your lawn with a regular routine of maintenance. Most fungi thrive in constant moisture, so water your lawn deeply yet infrequently. Thatch build-up aids in poor drainage and causes water runoff. Dethatch lawns with a thatch cutting machine as needed. Fertilize lawns monthly during their growing season. A healthy lawn will withstand fungus much better than an unhealthy one.

Disease Control

Unfortunately even the greenest and healthiest of lawns can become infested with a fungus disease. When this happens, there are two choices of control: cultural control and fungicidal control.

A cultural control is the best method of control. It includes all good practices of lawn maintenance: deep irrigation, weekly mowing, seasonal fertilizing, thatch removal, and annual weeding. Cultural control can sometimes stretch as far as pruning trees or moving shade-causing structures in order to admit more light to a shaded lawn.

A fungicidal control is the least desirable but often the surest type of control. It checks fungi and its progress only through the use of chemical treatments.

The chart that follows lists and describes the different lawn fungi, their symptoms, and how to treat them with either a cultural or a fungicidal control.

To apply fungicides, use the same type of mechanisms that you would use to apply weed killers and insecticides (see pages 20–22).

Check List of Physical Lawn Problems

Sometimes there are physical or mechanical problems in a lawn that cause it to look unhealthy. These conditions are usually permanent or repetitive, and they'll continue to cause trouble until you locate and correct them.

Here is a list of physical problems that can produce lawn troubles. But first, ask yourself these important questions: Have I fertilized the lawn lately? Am I watering it properly? If you're unsure, review the sections on watering (pages 10–11) and on fertilizing (pages 16–17).

Have you applied a chemical weed killer or pesticide in the last week? If spots appear in your lawn after chemicals have been applied, check whether the shape of the spots bears any relationship to the course you traveled with the dispenser or spreader. Spots that appear as streaks, squares, or half moons are probably chemical burns. Water the areas heavily to leach the excess chemicals into the ground. The lawn will eventually recover.

• **Has this spot persisted through all seasons for a year or so?** If it has, sight across the bad spots of the lawn to see if there are any high or low spots. Either of these physical features can bother grass—too much water in a low spot or too little water in a high spot. Fix the hill or dale by inserting a flat spade under the turf (2 or 3 inches below the surface), lifting it out in sections. If you have a low spot, fill in under the lifted area with enough enriched, conditioned soil to bring the turf section up to grade. Water, replace the turf sections, and water again. If you have a high spot, remove enough soil to bring the hump down to grade, replacing the sod, then water.

• **Does water stand on the surface or run off?** Compaction by traffic, a build-up of thatch beneath the grass, or just plain soil contrariness can be responsible for this condition. Open up the compacted area with a soil corer or aerator.

• **Perhaps your sprinkler system isn't giving enough water to the area.** Check the water dispersal (see page 11).

• **Are the bad spots in a shady area?** If the shade comes from trees, thin out the branches to let more light through; the grass will grow better. Feed lawns growing under a tree at least three times a year to replace the nutrients taken by the tree. Some trees are moisture robbers; try watering the grass around the tree more than the rest of the lawn. Cut grass higher under trees.

• **Do female dogs roam the premises?** They can be responsible for little dead spots often surrounded by a ring of very green grass. Soak the spots with water, and grass should begin to grow; if not, reseed the area.

• **The only remaining possibility is that something is wrong underground.** Use a soil corer or auger, a soil sampling tube, or a spade to dig down and find the problem. If there is some debris below, remove it. If there is a layer of hard clay, dig it out and replace it with good soil that is similar in texture to the soil above and below the clay layer. After you finish, make a seedbed over the area, sow new grass seed, and treat the spot like a new lawn (see pages 8–9) until the new grass is up and growing.

Lawn Diseases and Their Controls

Disease	Symptoms	Susceptible Grasses	Cultural Controls	Fungicidal Controls
Brown patch (*Rhizoctonia solani*)	Small, irregularly shaped brown spots that may enlarge as disease strengthens. Centers of spots may recover, exposing large brown circles (like smoke rings) in the lawn. Blades become water-soaked, turn yellowish brown, and die.	Bentgrasses Bermudas Bluegrasses Fescues Ryegrasses St. Augustine	Minimize shade. Aerate lawn. Irrigate 6 inches deep as needed. Avoid fertilizers high in nitrogen.	Benomyl Chlorothalonil PCNB Thiabendazole Thiophanate
Dollar spot (*Sclerotinia homeocarpa*)	Many small (approximately 2-inch) bleached or gray spots. When fungus first starts, infected areas have water-soaked appearance. Sometimes spots merge to make large, straw-colored areas. Dew-covered grass often reveals a cobwebby growth on the spots.	Bentgrasses Bermudas Bluegrasses Fescues Ryegrasses	Dethatch lawn. Irrigate 6 inches deep as needed. Apply a fertilizer high in nitrogen.	Anilazine Benomyl Chlorothalonil Thiabendazole Thiophanate
Fairy ring (*Marasmius oreades*)	Small circular patches of dark green grass, often followed by dead grass. Mushrooms may or may not be present.	All grasses	Aerate lawn. Apply a fertilizer high in nitrogen. Keep lawn wet for 3 to 5 days.	Sterilize the soil with methyl bromide. (This will kill lawns.)
Fusarium patch (*Fusarium nivale*)	Brown spots 2 to 12 inches in diameter. Look for weblike threads in grass thatch, or dead leaves. Same webby fungal threads can be seen on dew-covered grass.	Bluegrasses Creeping bentgrasses Fescues Ryegrasses Zoysia	Minimize shade. Aerate lawn. Improve drainage. Avoid fertilizers high in nitrogen.	Benomyl Chlorothalonil Thiabendazole (Apply in early fall.)
Grease spot (*Pythium*)	Infected blades turn dark and become matted together, giving a greasy appearance in streaks through the lawn. Sometimes a white cottony mold appears on leaf blades.	All grasses	Minimize shade. Aerate lawn. Irrigate 6 inches deep as needed.	Chloroneb Diazoben Ethazol
Melting out (*Helminthosporium vagans*)	A gradual, indefinite yellowing in the lawn. In infected areas, look for bright yellow leaf blades with brown spots and darkened borders. Eventually the whole leaf turns brown.	Kentucky bluegrass	Minimize shade. Aerate lawn. Improve drainage. Mow no shorter than 1¾ inches.	Anilazine Captan Chlorothalonil Cycloheximide Folpet
Red thread (*Coricium fuciforme*)	Spiderlike webs of pink thread bind blades together. Lawn yellows in patches 2 to 12 inches in diameter.	Bentgrasses Bluegrasses Fescues Ryegrasses	Apply a fertilizer high in nitrogen in late fall. Minimize shade.	Chlorothalonil Mancozeb
Rust (*Puccinia*)	Small reddish pustules form on older leaf blades and stems. Blades shrivel and die. Rub a white cloth over a suspected infection; if cloth picks up an orange color, it's rust.	Bluegrasses Ryegrasses	Apply a fertilizer high in nitrogen. Water regularly.	Maneb Oxycarboxin
Snow mold (*Typhula*)	Dirty white patches appear in the lawn. Margins between these patches are rather distinct. Dead grass pulls up easily. Most common in early spring when snow melts.	Bluegrasses Bentgrasses Fescues	Avoid applying fertilizers in late fall. Aerate lawn. Improve drainage. Mow frequently. Reduce snow pile-up.	Benomyl Thiabendazole Thiophanate (Apply before first snow.)

The Lawn Grasses

Your choice of a lawn grass will depend on your climate: there are two basic kinds of grasses—cool-season and subtropical—each with specific climate needs. The map on page 27 shows the rough division of the United States into these two grass regions.

Areas near the dividing line will be transitional, typically able to grow either type of lawn. If you are uncertain about which grasses will grow best in your area, look at your neighbors' lawns: the best-looking lawns will contain the grasses that perform well in your climate.

Some people will go to the extra time and expense of trying to maintain bluegrass, a cool-season grass, in a subtropical climate, probably because bluegrass is still considered by many to be the only true lawn grass. The most common and effective use of cool-season grasses in subtropical regions is to overseed subtropical grasses approaching dormancy in fall with certain cool-season grasses (see page 32). This keeps the lawn looking green in winter when the regular grasses turn brown.

Cool-season Grasses

The grasses that thrive in cool-season areas can withstand cold winters, but most types languish in hot summers.

Lawns of these grasses are usually started from seed; some are available as sod. Seeds come either in mixtures and blends of several different grasses or as individual types.

Lawns composed of a single grass type are the most uniform in appearance, giving you the maximum expression of whatever characteristic you select—a fine texture, for instance, or a tough play surface. The main disadvantage of a single-type grass lawn is that it could be wiped out if that one grass were susceptible to a pest or disease in your area or sensitive to a local environmental condition. A blend of several kinds of compatible grasses is safer.

Seed companies prepare grass seed blends for specific situations: for example, a fine-textured blend for an eye-pleasing lawn; several tough grasses for a play yard; or a mixture of low-light-tolerant grasses for shady areas. The types of grasses in the mature lawn may dwindle to one, two, or three kinds, but these will be the grasses that will do best with your particular soil, climate, and maintenance practices.

If you are unsure of the type of grass you want or the best blend for your area, the three best sources of information are a large, reputable garden center, your County Cooperative Extension Advisor (or agricultural agent) (look in the white pages of your telephone book under your county listing), and gardeners with good-looking lawns in your neighborhood. Garden centers should carry the grass seed and blends that will perform best in your particular climate. Be sure to point out any specific problems your lawn will have, such as heavy shade or heavy use. The grasses recommended by garden center personnel will be the ones that have proved dependable and the least troublesome in your area.

A tour of your neighborhood will help you locate lawns that meet your requirements and are well suited to your particular climate. Once you have found a healthy-looking lawn, ask its owner which type or blend of grasses it represents and how he or she maintains it. (Even if you planted the same turf, without adequate maintenance it just wouldn't have the same appearance.)

Buy your seed first on the basis of the kind of lawn you want, and second on the cost required to cover your area rather than on the cost per pound. Choice, fine-leafed blends contain more seeds per pound than coarse, fast-growing blends (the seeds of fine-textured blends are much smaller). So a pound of fine-leafed grass seeds will cover a greater area than a pound of larger seeds. For more information on how to purchase grass seeds, see page 29.

If you live in a dry climate where drought is a possibility, see the special section on page 30 that covers drought-resistant grasses.

Bluegrasses

Kentucky bluegrass is probably the most important cool-season grass; rough-stalked bluegrass may be used in shade blends; and annual bluegrass is usually considered a weed. The grass blades of all bluegrasses have a characteristic boat-shaped tip.

Kentucky bluegrass (*Poa pratensis*). Kentucky bluegrass forms a rich, blue green lawn grass in areas with mild summers and ample water. Many types are available in seed or sod. Some forms you may encounter are Merion, Baron, Park, Adelphi, Rugby, Parade, Fylking, or Victa.

Bluegrass needs ample water and a minimum of one fertilizing in spring and one in fall. Mow high—1½ to 2 inches—leaving plenty of leaf blade to feed the plant and shade the root zone. Fusarium blight may occur during summer heat. If your grass is deep rooted, irrigate deeply so that the soil is moist to a depth of at least 4 to 6 inches. With a sparse or shallow-rooted lawn, you may need to supplement the deep watering with short morning waterings almost daily.

Rough-stalked bluegrass (*Poa trivialis*). This is a fine-textured, bright green grass that is sometimes used in shady lawn mixtures. It tolerates low light levels and damp soil. It grows wild outside shady areas and can become a weed in wet spots.

Annual bluegrass (*Poa annua*). The bright green, soft-textured grass is an undependable annual that grows mostly during the cool months of the year. It's likely to leave bare spots in your summer lawn. It also produces seed heads borne on top of the grass that give the turf an overall white-flecked appearance. To discourage annual bluegrass, maintain a thick-turfed, deep-rooted lawn.

Annual bluegrass can behave like a perennial grass in shady, wet areas. If you want to maintain it as turf, mow it regularly to reduce seed heads.

Fescue grasses

Fescues come in many forms. Lawn fescues are generally classified as fine or coarse.

Red fescue (*Festuca rubra*). A fine-bladed grass used in seed mixtures with bluegrass or other lawn grasses, red fescue has narrow, fine-textured,

Grasses and Climate

About 1,500 different kinds of grasses grow in the United States. This figure includes pasture grasses, range grasses, and other members of the grass family as diverse as bamboo, corn, and sugar cane.

Of all these grasses, only about 40 types are usually cultivated as lawns. Several of these cultivated grasses have numerous strains or varieties that have been developed to give you a multitude of choices. Many of these newer strains or varieties have been developed to be disease resistant or more adaptable to different climates.

Grasses have these anatomical points in common: Leaves grow alternately in two rows up the sides of the jointed stems. The space between the joints may be hollow or pithy. A sheath surrounds the stem above each joint. Follow the sheath up the stem, and you come to a collarlike growth (called the "auricle") that clasps the stem at the top of the sheath. The blade grows outward, and usually upward, from this collar.

The particular arrangement of sheath, auricle, and blade helps botanists and grass seed growers identify lawn grasses in the absence of flowers or a seedspike. Other aids to identification include the shape of the leaves, thickness of the stem, color, and the means of spreading—stolons or underground stems known as rhizomes.

Grass blades elongate from the lower end, so that when you mow off the tips, the leaves renew their length from the root end or new blades sprout from the base. This characteristic is what makes grasses uniquely adapted for use as a close-cropped ground cover.

The map below divides the United States into two major grass-growing climates. The cool-season grasses grow best to the north of the line, the subtropical grasses south of the line. The shaded area immediately around the line is called the transition zone. In many cases gardeners who live in the transition zone can grow either type grass. Cool-season grasses are described on pages 26, 28; subtropical grasses on pages 28, 31–32.

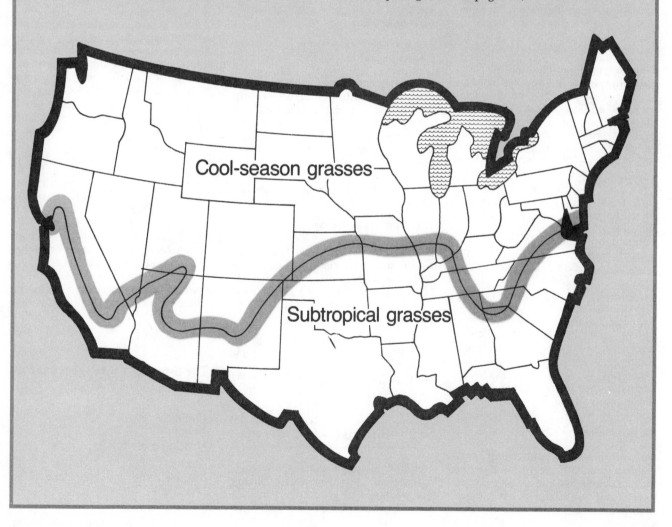

Cool-season grasses

Subtropical grasses

dark green blades. It tends to grow in clumps if planted alone.

This grass will tolerate almost any type soil, some drought, and some shade, but not blazing sun. Mow it at 1½ to 2 inches tall for best performance. It can be used to overseed Bermuda grass lawns in winter and will not compete with emerging Bermuda grass in spring.

Common red fescue may also be called creeping red fescue. It's the most shade tolerant of the good lawn grasses. Other varieties include Creeping Red, 'Illahee', 'Pennlawn', and 'Rainier'.

Sheep fescue, hard fescue. Sheep fescue (*Festuca ovina*) is a fine, needle-bladed, low-growing, clumping grass that tolerates dry or poor soil. Hard fescue (*Festuca ovina duriuscula*) makes a better lawn grass. The variety 'Biljart' has a blue green color that blends well with bluegrass.

Blue fescue (*Festuca ovina glauca*) is a useful ground cover for sunny or partially shady areas (For further information, see page 71.)

Chewings fescue (*Festuca rubra commutata*). This grass also tends to clump. Unmowed, it makes an attractive meadow grass on steep slopes.

Tall fescue (*Festuca elatior*). This clumping grass is used for erosion control or for rough-textured lawns, such as athletic fields. The tough blades will grow in compacted soil. It forms no runners, so plant seeds closely for a dense turf. Sow 8 to 10 pounds of seed per 1,000 square feet in fall.

To keep a tall fescue lawn looking lush, fertilize lightly (about ½ pound of actual nitrogen per 1,000 square feet of lawn) once a month in summer, one or more times in fall, and again in early spring if you live in a mild climate. In a cold-winter climate, wait until all danger of frost has passed before the spring application. Tall fescue does best mowed at 2 inches.

Forms for use in home lawns include: 'Alta', coarse, tough; 'Fawn', narrowest-leafed form, fine textured; 'Goars', tolerates saline or alkaline soil; 'Kentucky 31' (may be called K-31), good in hot-summer climates, in transition zones in the South.

Bent grasses

All bent grasses except redtop make velvety lawns if grown under the proper conditions and given constant care. They need frequent close mowing, frequent fertilizing, lots of water,

and an occasional top dressing. In hot weather, fungus diseases can be troublesome.

In northern climates, bent grasses tend to dominate bluegrasses and fescues.

Creeping bent (*Agrostis stolonifera* and *A. s. palustris*). This form of bent grass creates the best turf for golf greens, but it needs the most care, including mowing from ¼ to ½ inch high with a special mower.

Seed-grown strains include Emerald, Penncross, and Seaside. You may also find sod of varieties called Congressional and Old Orchard.

Colonial bent (*Agrostis tenuis*). Commonly grown in New England, the Pacific Northwest, and the coastal region of Northern California, this bent grass is more erect and easier to care for than the creeping bents. Mow it at a ¾-inch height.

Plant Astoria along the seacoast, Highland inland. Highland tolerates hot weather.

Redtop (*Agrostis gigantea*). This bent grass is a coarser grass, not generally used in lawns.

Rye grasses

While not considered a choice lawn grass in the past, today rye grass can be useful, expecially some of the newly developed forms. Plants tend to clump instead of forming runners. Ryegrass may be used in low-cost blends to cover large areas and is often used to overseed subtropical lawns because it germinates and establishes itself quickly.

Perennial rye (*Lolium perenne*). A deep green, glossy, fast-sprouting grass, perennial rye grows in clumps. Flower and seed stems may lie under reel-type mower blades. 'Manhattan' is a fine-textured, uniform grass. Other forms are 'Pennfine', 'Derby', 'Regal', and 'Loretta'.

Italian or annual ryegrass. This very coarse grass is used as a winter cover for soil erosion on bare soil or to overseed dormant subtropical lawns.

Subtropical Grasses

Unlike cool-season grasses, subtropical grasses grow vigorously during hot weather and go dormant in cool or cold winters. If you find their win-

ter brownness offensive, you can either overseed them with certain annual cool-season grasses (see page 32) or dye them green to provide green color during mild winters (grass dye may not be available in some areas). Even in their winter brown or straw-colored stage, subtropical grasses maintain a carpet that keeps mud from being tracked into your house. In very mild-winter climates, these grasses may stay green all year with adequate nitrogen fertilizer.

Many subtropical grasses are grown from stolons, sprigs, plugs, or sod (see page 7 for planting instructions). Common Bermuda, U-3 Bermuda, Bahia, and Zoysia japonica may be available as seed; seeding is generally unsatisfactory for Zoysia japonica, and the seeds aren't widely offered.

Hybrid Bermuda grasses, Bahia, and St. Augustine grass cover quickly with runners, while centipede grass and the zoysias are relatively slow to cover. Once established in a dense turf, these grasses can crowd out broad-leafed weeds. Hybrid Bermudas require frequent mowing and frequent attention to thatch removal.

Most subtropical grasses are vigorous, invasive growers, so you may need some type of edging to contain them: wooden edging (use redwood or cedar if available, or use pressure-treated wood), concrete curbing, or a brick or concrete block edging should keep grasses out of the flower beds. These edgings can also serve as mowing strips.

Mowing heights for subtropical grasses vary according to climate. From the Southeast through Texas, mowing heights also vary by season. The following lists include recommended mowing heights for the Southeast area through Texas and mowing heights for the Southwest and California. For the Southeast through Texas, the listed heights apply to mowing in spring and fall: during the summer months, add ½ inch to these heights.

The Southeast through Texas

Grass type	Mowing height
Common Bermuda	1 inch
Hybrid Bermudas	½ inch
Zoysias	¾ inch
St. Augustine Centipede	1½ inches
Bahia	2½ inches

(Continued on page 31)

How to Read a Grass Seed Label

The label on a grass seed package is your key in choosing a high quality seed. It can also help you avoid a product that could actually damage your lawn.

The label shown below describes a typical cool-season grass seed mixture. Here's what you should look for:

Grass Seed Type

The type of lawn you want will determine which type of grass seed you select. If you want a fine-textured, picture-perfect lawn, look for a mixture in which fine-textured grasses account for more than 50 percent of the mix. Whenever coarse-textured grass is included in a mix, it should be at least 40 percent of the total—otherwise your lawn will not have an even texture. If you want a rough-and-tumble lawn for children or adults to play on, you'll want even more coarse-type grass.

Improved variety grasses will be named: these varieties have been specially developed for good color, texture, or disease resistance, and are your best value. Germination rates for all types of grass should be given.

Other Ingredients

The items listed under this heading are potential problem makers. "Crop" is usually listed first as a problem ingredient. Legally, crop is anything that is grown commercially by a farmer. Crop can be more of a problem in a lawn than weeds, since any chemical control you might use to kill it could kill your grass, too.

Crop can also include other turf grasses that might spoil the color or texture of your lawn. Look for the lowest possible percentage of crop in your grass mix.

"Inert matter" simply means filler—chaff, ground corn cobs, leaves, or even sand. Again, a low percentage of inert matter means a better value seed.

"Weed seed" is just that—seeds for plants that don't belong in your lawn. Again, the lower the percentage of weed seed, the better. Every grass seed package will contain a few weed seeds because of the harvesting techniques used in producing the seeds, but most of these weeds can't tolerate regular mowing and will be eradicated in a few months.

What's in a Pound?

Some consumers judge grass seed package value by the price per pound. But since lawn grass seeds can vary considerably in size, your best guide to value is the number of square feet the package will cover. A pound of most species of bluegrass seed will contain five times as many seeds as a pound of ryegrass seed.

Don't try to get a bargain when you buy grass seed. Most people expect a lawn to last from 15 to 20 years or longer, so you should buy the best quality seed you can find to give your lawn a good start.

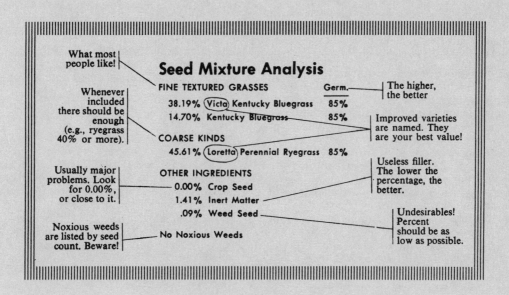

The Drought-tolerant Grasses

If you deal with drought conditions on a regular basis, you know that maintaining a healthy, green lawn isn't easy. But you can turn the situation around by planting a drought-tolerant grass, giving it proper care, and using available water prudently.

The low-water-consuming turf plants are divided into two groups: the hardy cool-season grasses that you grow from seed sown in October (most of these stay green all year), and the subtropical turf grasses that you start in spring from stolons, sprigs, plugs, or sod (all of these turn brown in winter). Whichever drought-tolerant grass you choose, you will need to properly prepare the seedbed before you plant. Soil preparation instructions are given on pages 8–9.

Cool-season Drought-tolerant Grasses

In general, the grasses that can stand up to drought look coarser than Kentucky bluegrass. There are two basic types: the tall fescues that are used mostly at low elevations, and the high-elevation grasses that thrive in the Rocky Mountains.

The tall fescues. You can choose from four varieties of tall fescue (*Festuca arundinacea*): Alta (medium-coarse texture, very wear-resistant); Fawn (narrowest-leaf form); Goars (toughest in texture, tolerates saline and alkaline soils); and Kentucky 31 (sometimes called K-31, grows well in warm-summer climates). All varieties grow well in sun or semishade and survive winter temperatures down to about 20° F. Plant these fescues at 8–10 pounds of seed per 1,000 square feet of lawn.

If it hasn't rained, and the seedlings are 2 or 3 inches high, give the grass a heavy soaking. Try to penetrate at least 12 inches deep. Thereafter, water the same amount whenever the leaf blades begin to fold or curve. Fertilize lightly once a month in summer and three times more in fall and winter. Mow the tall fescues 2 inches high.

The high-elevation grasses. Lawn planters in the arid alkaline regions of the Rocky Mountains and high plains have four choices in drought-tolerant grasses: buffalo grass (*Buchloe dactyloides*), blue grama (*Bouteloua gracilis*), Western wheatgrass (*Agropyron smithii*), and the fairway variety of crested wheatgrass (*Agropyron cristatum* 'Fairway'). These grasses can be seeded either in October or in spring.

Buffalo grass thrives in hot-summer climates and takes winter cold down to −20° F. Unfortunately, it is very aggressive, readily invading surrounding garden beds. Sow 2 pounds of seed per 1,000 square feet of lawn and allow about 28 days for seeds to germinate. Soak to depth of 12 inches until the grass is established; then the grass needs only three waterings during the dry season.

Blue grama grass tolerates 110° F. in summer and down to −40° in winter. It isn't invasive. Sow 1 pound of seed per 1,000 square feet. Soak to a depth of 12 inches until blue grama is established; then it can survive with no irrigation. Mow it to a height of 1½ inches. It is not readily available.

Western wheatgrass and crested wheatgrass can handle temperatures as high as 110° F. and as low as −20°. Plant these grasses at a rate of 2 pounds per 1,000 square feet. Germination takes 14–28 days. Once the grass is established, soak it 18–20 inches deep every 30 days if there are no rains. Mow wheat grass to 2 inches high.

Subtropical Drought-tolerant Grasses

Three types of subtropical grasses are generally drought-tolerant: the Bermudas, Zoysia grasses, and St. Augustine grass. All turn brownish in winter.

All subtropical grasses do best in warm climates. They survive temperatures down to 20° F. and thrive in summer highs of 110°. Fertilize all of these grasses with a high-nitrogen fertilizer at least once in fall and once in winter. In summer, fertilize at 6-week intervals.

The Bermudas. These grasses need the least amount of water because of their deep roots. Plant either by sod or stolons (4–6 bushels of stolons per 1,000 square feet). Mow Bermuda grass as low as possible.

St. Augustine grass. Plant from sod, stolons (6 bushels per 1,000 square feet), or plugs. To plant plugs from flats, use 10 flats per 1,000 square feet, placing 2-inch plugs in rows about 10 inches apart. (Plug planting is discussed on page 37.) Keep the ground moist until grass is established.

Zoysia grasses. These grasses need warm nights for best growth. They are commonly planted from plugs or stolons. Allow 10–14 months for grass to fill in.

Watering Tips

If you live in an area with little water, a sprinkler system can be useful if it functions well and completely covers your lawn area. Run the system at night or in early morning when it's windless and cool, and water pressure is best.

Pull all weeds from your lawn quickly. This will not only save your lawn's appearance, but it will save water as well. For weeds that are too numerous or too tough-rooted to pull, use a selective weed killer.

California and the Southwest
(year-round heights)

Grass type	Mowing height
Common Bermuda	¾ inch
Hybrid Bermudas	¼ to ½ inch
St. Augustine	¾ to 1½ inches

One cool-season grass—tall fescue, especially the variety 'Kentucky 31'—is commonly grown in the transitional areas of the subtropical Southeast, such as parts of Virginia and Tennessee, and cold-winter areas of North and South Carolina and Georgia. For information on growing tall fescue, see page 28.

Bermuda grasses

Bermuda grass (*Cynodon dactylon*) is a subtropical, medium to fine-textured grass that spreads rapidly by surface and underground runners. It can tolerate heat and needs less water than most lawn grasses, but careful maintenance is needed to keep it looking its best. It prefers full sun and should be mowed low (see mowing chart above and on page 28).

Bermudas can go dormant in winter (the grass turns brown); some varieties will remain green longer than others, especially if well fertilized. Bermuda grass can be overseeded in fall with cool-season grasses such as rye or red fescue, or it can be dyed green for winter color.

Thatch can be a maintenance problem. Thatch is a matted layer of old stems and stolons that forms beneath the grass blades; a thick thatch could impair proper drainage and plant growth. Thatch should be removed annually. Thatching techniques are discussed on page 32.

To plant stolons, scatter them evenly by hand over the prepared planting area (see pages 8–9) and roll with a cleated roller (available at most nurseries that sell stolons). If you can't find a cleated roller, sprinkle a fine layer of topsoil over the stolons.

If the area is small, you could plant the stolons individually, 6 inches apart. Make a small hole, put one end of a stolon in it, and press the soil back around it with your hand, foot, or a flat-bladed tool such as a trowel.

Whichever method you use, fertilize the area, then sprinkle the surface with water when planting is com-

plete. Keep the area moist until the stolons start growing.

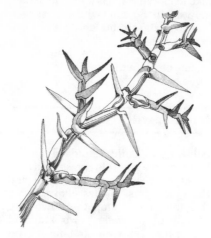

Bermuda stolons are pieces of grass stem (shown) cut in 1 or 2-inch pieces, each with a few tufts of green.

Common Bermuda is a low-maintenance grass for large areas. It needs some fertilizing (at least twice a year—spring and fall) and careful and frequent mowing. Its root system can invade shrubbery and flower beds if not confined, and it's difficult to eradicate. Plant common Bermuda by seed.

Hybrid Bermudas have a finer texture and better color than common Bermuda. To keep the grass green longer into winter you can fertilize in September and October.

Remove thatch from late spring through summer when grass is growing vigorously.

To establish hybrid Bermudas, roll out sod (see page 7) or plant stolons just as you would plant seed—by hand casting at the rate of 4 to 6 bushels per 1,000 square feet.

Some varieties you may encounter include 'Santa Ana', deep green, coarse blades if mowed high, holds color late, smog resistant, takes hard wear; 'Tifgreen', fine textured, deep green, dense, takes close mowing, good for putting greens, outstanding for home lawns; 'Tifway', low growth, fine textured, stiff blades, dark green, dense, takes hard use, slow to start; 'Tifdwarf', extremely low and dense, takes very close mowing, slower to establish than other forms, slower to spread, good in small areas.

St. Augustine grass

St. Augustine (*Stenotaphrum secundatum*) is a tropical or subtropical

coarse-textured grass that spreads rapidly by surface runners that root at joints. The blades are dark green, up to ⅜ inch wide, on coarse, wiry stems.

St. Augustine tolerates much wear, has few pest problems (except for chinch bugs), is fairly salt tolerant, and endures shade better than other subtropical grasses. It does turn brown during short winter dormancy and produces a thick thatch which needs attention.

St. Augustine does creep into flower beds and other plantings including neighboring lawns, but it is easily removed because of its shallow root system. Some type of edging can help contain it.

Plant from sod (see page 7), stolons, or plugs. Plant stolons at the rate of 6 bushels per 1,000 square feet, following directions given for Bermuda on this page. To plant plugs (you'll need 10 flats per 1,000 square feet), cut 2-inch plugs (see page 37, or pull pieces apart and place them in rows about 10 inches apart. Keep the ground very moist until sprouts grow, then reduce watering.

Zoysia grasses

Zoysia lawn grasses tend to spread slowly on creeping rhizomes and need warm nights for best growth. They are fairly deep rooted, drought tolerant, and long lived. They go dormant and turn straw-colored during cold weather, and they tend to stay brown longer than other subtropical grasses.

Zoysias are commonly planted from plugs or stolons; some sod is available. Follow the same planting procedures given for Bermuda grasses, and allow 10 to 14 months for grass to fill in.

Zoysia japonica. It's best known variety is 'Meyer'. It is coarser than other zoysias with broad, stiff blades.

Zoysia matrella. This fine-textured, bright green grass, called 'Flawn', makes an attractive turf that spreads very slowly in coastal California's cool-night climates. It spreads faster in warmer regions, but is slower than bermudas. It is relatively pest free and tolerates some shade. It withstands hard wear.

Zoysia 'Emerald' is a hybrid between *Z. japonica* and *Z. tenuifolia* (Korean velvetgrass), a hardy, fine-textured ground cover. 'Emerald' is vigorous, making a dense, bright green carpet in one summer when planted from 1-inch plugs set 9 inches apart.

(Continued on page 32)

Centipede grass

Centipede (*Eremochloa ophiuroides*) spreads moderately fast on thick, creeping stems. It grows well in the Southeast and in Hawaii and requires less maintenance than most subtropical grasses, but may be damaged by salt spray. It is drought resistant, but it performs better with regular waterings during hot, dry weather.

Centipede needs very little fertilizer; once or twice a year is sufficient. Too much feeding will eventually kill it. If grass begins to yellow, it is probably iron deficient; treat it for chlorosis (see page 6).

To plant centipede, use stolons or plugs (see pages 31 and 37). Seed may be available, but isn't dependable.

Bahia grass

Bahia (*Paspalum notatum*) is a low-growing, coarse grass that spreads by runners. It forms an easy-to-care-for turf in southern coastal areas, but has unattractive seedheads.

Common Bahia is a pasture grass. Finer-leafed strains, such as Paraguay and Argentine, make good lawn turf in either sun or partial shade. Bahia tends to stay green longer in winter than other subtropical grasses.

Two or three fertilizer applications in early spring and fall are sufficient.

Pensacola Bahiagrass can be combined with tall fescue to make an evergreen turf of uniform appearance. Plant 3 pounds of Bahia seed and 6 pounds of fescue seed per 1,000 square feet of lawn area.

Related to Bahia, other tropical grasses (forms of *Paspalum vaginatum*) are now available in parts of Southern California and Arizona. Labeled Fu-turf, 'Adelaide', or Adelayd, these grasses are more glossy green than Bermuda grass, and where winters are mild, they may stay green all year. They have shallow roots and will need water more often than Bermuda. Fertilize them as you would Bahia grass.

These grasses may be sold as sod or rhizomes. The best mowing height is between ¼ and ½ inch.

Overseeding

In late October or early November, many turf gardeners camouflage the winter brownness of their Bermuda grass lawns by overseeding. Annual ryegrass, perennial rye, or red fescue can be used as winter grass.

To overseed, mow your lawn as low as possible, rake it with a flexible steel rake to loosen runners and thatch, then mow again. Sow the winter grass seed (you can lightly mulch it) and keep the lawn moist until the seeds germinate. Mow the winter grass to 1½ inches or higher.

Dealing with Thatch

A lawn may build up a dead-looking layer of thatch—old grass and stolons—between the soil surface and the green grass blades above. Often this thatch will stop the downward movement of water. Two kinds of thatch may cause you trouble: a layer of matted clippings made by mowing tall grass without a grass catcher, and a thicker, more springy layer of old stems and stolons beneath the green grass blades, caused by the natural growth pattern of your grass mixture.

You can usually scratch matted clippings out with a rake. To prevent their formation, use a grass catcher, mow often enough so the clippings will be short, or cross mow to chop up the cuttings into shorter lengths. In the eastern United States, thatch buildup may be caused by too frequent fertilizing.

Opening up a thatch of interwoven stolons and stems can be difficult. If the thatch isn't too bad, you can mow grass low, rake with a flexible steel rake, then repeat the process. Or you can rent a machine especially designed to handle thatch removal.

Available at most equipment rental stores, these machines have revolving vertical knives that slice down through the grass and thatch to the soil. They leave enough rooted grass plants so the lawn can recuperate quickly. But they also comb out great quantities of dead material and once again open up the stolon mat so water can reach the soil.

Dethatching with a machine has a definitely weakening effect on lawn grass, so be sure the thatch buildup warrants it. Keep in mind that this procedure is not a cure-all for poor lawn care. Most experts recommend that machine dethatching be done not more than once every 3 years.

When to dethatch. Timing for machine dethatching (also called renovating) can be crucial; it depends on your climate and grass type.

For California and the southern states, bluegrass lawns can be de-

thatched in spring or fall (fall being preferable). If you renovate in fall, do it early enough so there's still at least a month of good growing weather so the grass can recuperate. For Bermuda grass lawns, late spring or summer is the best time.

In the midwestern and eastern states, either spring or fall is good timing. Again, fall is the preferred season; be sure to renovate early enough to leave a month of good growing weather.

In the Pacific Northwest, fall and early spring are recommended times for dethatching. Spring is considered the best time in this area because the long growing season is ahead.

Aerating Your Lawn

Compacted soil can be opened up by aerating tools that remove small cores of earth. You can get a two, three, or four-tube aerator that you push into the ground with your foot. You can get a small weighted mobile aerator in which the coring tubes are arranged on a wheel that you push back and forth. If you have a large area, you may want to rent or hire a machine-operated aerator.

One problem you may encounter is that the dirt can be so compacted that you can't get the aerator into the soil more than about an inch. To solve this problem, water the area slowly up to its capacity the day before. Aerate the area to whatever depth you can, then run a sprinkler over the area at low pressure until the soil is at capacity again. After the soil has dried enough to lose all stickiness, repeat the aeration. The first pass with the aerator should have opened the ground so the water can soften the soil.

You can aerate a compacted area and leave the holes open; grass roots will fill it in. But since you know your soil tends to pack down, you can rake a top dressing into the area to help lighten the soil. A good top dressing contains between 50 and 100 percent fine sand (not ocean sand). If your soil isn't too clayey, let the plugged cores sit until they become crumbly; then mix fine sand with the crumbled cores, and brush or rake the mixture into the holes.

The practice of driving a fork into the ground instead of an aerating tool is not recommended. The fork is likely to make the condition worse by compacting the soil at each point where the tines enter it.

Perennial ryegrass 'Derby'
Perennial rye is a deep green, glossy, clumping grass (see page 28).

Bluegrass Adelphi
Kentucky bluegrass forms a rich, blue green lawn (see page 26).

Tall fescue 'Alta'
A coarse, clumping grass, tall fescue is for rough use (see pages 26, 28).

The Cool-season Grasses

Creeping bentgrass Emerald
If given lots of care, bent grasses make velvety lawns (see page 28).

Cool-season grass seed mixture called Golden Gate blend combines perennial ryegrass, red fescue, and bluegrass seeds for a lawn with an even texture and consistent color. Cool-season grasses are discussed on pages 26–28.

'Tifgreen' hybrid Bermuda grass creates this velvety lawn in subtropical climates. 'Tifgreen' is one of the newer hybrids that are less aggressive than older types, have fewer seed heads to mar the even texture, and hold their green color longer into winter. Bermuda grasses and other subtropical grasses are discussed on pages 28, 31, and 32.

The Subtropical Grasses

Bermuda grass 'Santa Ana'
Hybrid Bermudas make lawns with
fine texture, good color (see page 31).

Common Bermuda grass
Common Bermuda is a low-maintenance, invasive grass (see page 31).

Zoysia 'Emerald'
Zoysia forms a dense, vigorous, bright
green lawn (see page 31).

St. Augustine grass Texas Common
Coarse-textured St. Augustine spreads
rapidly (see page 31).

Centipede grass
Centipede makes a coarse-textured,
drought-tolerant turf (see pages 31–32).

Paspalum grass 'Adelaide'
This paspalum is a glossy green grass
related to Bahia (see page 32).

Dichondra lawn features smooth, even texture, consistent color usually associated with turf grass. Dichondra requires mild-winter climates, infrequent mowing.

Close-up of dichondra leaves shows how tiny, irregularly rounded, dark green leaves overlap to form dense cover.

The Dichondra Lawn

Dichondra (*Dichondra micrantha*, also called *D. carolinensis* or *D. repens*) is a soft, green, ground-hugging, broad-leafed plant that is widely grown as a lawn in the mild-winter areas of California and Arizona. It can be used as a turf plant in most areas where winter temperatures don't drop below 25° F., and it has been successful in a few slightly colder climates.

Dichondra produces a mat of small, round leaves that resemble miniature water lily pads. It spreads by rooting surface runners and also may reseed itself naturally. Planted in sunny areas or in areas that get regular heavy foot traffic, dichondra stays low and tight. Grown in the shade with little foot traffic and ample fertilizer, it can reach as high as 6 inches with a lush, uneven appearance.

It will grow well in southeastern states but is seldom cultivated there. Several southern agricultural extension services list the native larger-leafed form (*D. carolinensis*) as a lawn weed called ponyfoot.

Planting Dichondra

Dichondra can be grown from plugs or seed. The amount you plant determines how quickly you get coverage. Two pounds of seed for each 1,000 square feet will give you a lawn in 5 weeks; one pound will give you a lawn in 6 to 7 weeks. One ounce of seed would cover in several years, but the longer you have bare ground, the greater the weed problem will be.

The best time to sow dichondra is from March through May; midsummer plantings will germinate faster but will need careful, frequent waterings. Planting early will produce sturdy root systems that can take midsummer heat and some water stress.

Prepare the seed bed as you would for a new grass lawn (see pages 8–9). Dichondra seeds sown in spring need no mulching; just rake the seed gently and roll it with a light roller. If you sow in summer, use a light mulch of damp peat moss—enough to cover—to help keep the seedbed moist.

Plug planting, once the only way to establish dichondra, is still practical for small areas such as between steppingstones, for banks or slopes, or for an immediate lawnlike effect. Plugs also require a thoroughly prepared seedbed.

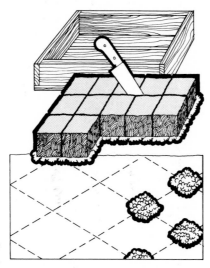

Turn flat of dichondra upside down and, using a sharp knife, cut like a sheet cake into 1 or 2-inch squares.

Plugs should be no smaller than 1 inch square—2-inch-square plugs or larger will give you faster coverage and less transplanting shock. Turn a dichondra flat over on a level surface and cut through the soil with a sharp knife or saw (see illustration above). Plant the plugs in an offset grid pattern 6 to 12 inches apart—keep in mind that the closer plugs are placed, the faster the coverage will be. Make sure any runners are set at soil level or just below; then tap the plug in gently.

Caring for Dichondra Lawns

Dichondra needs as much care as most grass lawns for a neat appearance. It needs regular, thorough waterings to maintain a deep root system, especially during hot weather. It also prefers frequent light fertilizing: fertilize with the lightest application recommended on the fertilizer's label, once every 2 to 3 weeks.

Depending on what you want your dichondra lawn to look like, you can mow it frequently, seldom, or not at all. Grown in full sun and given lots of use, dichondra stays low and even, needing mowing infrequently if ever. Dichondra grown in the shade or given little use may need frequent mowings to give it an even appearance.

Mowing at ¾-inch height (higher during hot weather to avoid stress) will encourage a small-leafed, even dichondra lawn, but you will need to mow it regularly. You can mow at a 1½ to 2-inch height more infrequently; this will promote a less consistent texture and leaves of varying sizes.

If you mow dichondra too close, you'll get a scalped look; top dress it with a light mulch to help it come back.

Dichondra Woes

Dichondra and grasses share an equal number of problems. Many of the same pests attack both types of lawn, so use the controls discussed on pages 22–23.

Dichondra flea beetle can devastate dichondra lawns. The first signs of the disease are browning leaves with engraved lines where tissue has been gnawed. To control, apply diazinon as soon as possible, following label directions carefully.

The best weed control is simply to keep your dichondra lawn growing so luxuriantly that weeds can't get a root hold. If you do find weeds, handpull them before they have a chance to spread.

If weeds do become a problem, you can find weed-killing compounds specially formulated for use on specific dichondra lawn weeds. It's very important to follow the label directions exactly, as dichondra can be considered a broad-leafed weed, and general broad-leafed weed chemicals would also kill dichondra. Further information on weed identification and controls appears on pages 20–21.

Ground Covers

For a Variety of Landscape Situations

Many gardeners have places in their landscape that need
some low-growing plants. But what if these areas are
unsuitable for lawn grasses? Or what if the gardener just prefers
a different look than turf provides? This is the time to turn
to the beauty and versatility of the ground covers.
You can choose, for example, a ground-hugging mat of
creeping thyme or Irish moss, or a lush, billowy bed of baby's
tears or ivy. And many ground covers offer a seasonal
bonus—flowers to splash color across any part of the garden.
This section covers general techniques for watering and
planting ground covers, shows how these plants adapt to a
wide variety of situations such as steep hillsides or deep
shade, and includes a comprehensive listing of low-growing
plants suitable for use as ground covers.

Ways to Water Ground Covers

When it comes to water, ground covers are individuals. The amount of water you will need to provide depends on your plants' specific needs, your climate (mild, humid, or dry), your soil (clay or sandy), and the location of the planting (sun or shade). You will find watering instructions for each plant in the ground covers listing, pages 56–95.

Watering with Sprinklers

If your ground cover needs water on a regular basis or your planting is rather large, you may want to install a sprinkler system. It should be installed at the soil preparation stage before planting as explained on pages 14–15.

Sprinkler heads should be set on risers so they will sit a few inches above the mature established plants; risers also produce a rainlike effect.

Approximate heights for established ground covers are given in the individual plant listings, pages 56–95.

To achieve the same effect with portable sprinkler units (see page 13),

you can elevate them on wooden blocks or bricks.

Watering by Hand

If you plan to water with a hose, make your watering simpler by using one of the hand nozzles pictured. Choose a nozzle that can be adjusted to apply water in a mist or light spray. Nozzles such as the pistol type that produce hard bursts of water are helpful in washing off dusty foliage or pest infestations. Soakers provide a slow trickle of water that won't gouge holes in the soil around the roots.

Providing a Watering Basin

If you water by hand and your ground covers are at least a foot apart, plants can benefit from individual watering basins until they fill in. A watering basin is a low circular dike of soil built up just outside the plant's drip line (the circle beneath the plant's outer leaves where most rainwater drips to the ground). You can place a

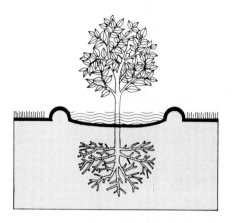

soaker inside the basin and let the water slowly penetrate the soil. Roots will have time to absorb the moisture because the plant's foliage shades the basin, reducing evaporation. You can use the same basin to fertilize the plant.

Seven Soakers

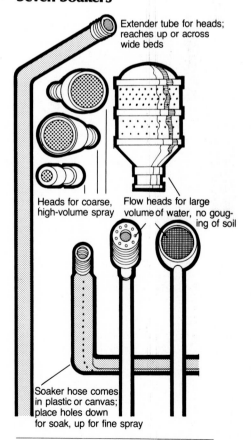

Extender tube for heads; reaches up or across wide beds

Heads for coarse, high-volume spray

Flow heads for large volume of water, no gouging of soil

Soaker hose comes in plastic or canvas; place holes down for soak, up for fine spray

Hose-end Nozzles for Specific Watering Jobs

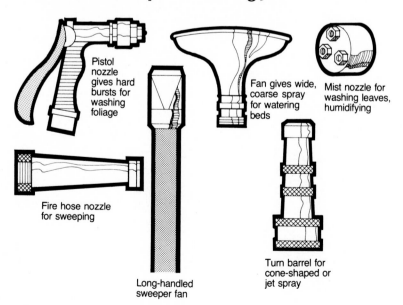

Pistol nozzle gives hard bursts for washing foliage

Fire hose nozzle for sweeping

Long-handled sweeper fan

Fan gives wide, coarse spray for watering beds

Mist nozzle for washing leaves, humidifying

Turn barrel for cone-shaped or jet spray

Planting Techniques for Ground Covers

Since most ground covers are planned and planted as a permanent part of the landscape, providing a good growing environment in the beginning is worth the extra effort. Before you actually put your ground cover in the soil, you should consider several things: the kind of soil you have, the kind of soil your particular ground cover needs, and the amount of water it will require.

If you've chosen a ground cover that will need more water than your climate produces naturally, some method for delivering water on a routine basis should be included in your landscape plan. Should you decide to install an irrigation system, do it at the soil preparation stage. Various watering techniques and systems are discussed on pages 10–15 and 39.

Preparing the Soil

You can approach the matter of soil preparation in one of two ways—either improve the entire planting area (as you would for a new lawn installation) or improve just the soil in and around each individual planting hole. To improve an area that is fairly large and not too steep, follow the steps used for lawn installations (see pages 8–9) up to the leveling and rolling phases.

If you've chosen a low-growing, soil-hugging cover such as *Ajuga* or *Thymus*, you may want to include the leveling and rolling steps as well. For instructions on improving the soil in each planting hole, see "Ground covers in nursery containers," on page 41.

Methods of Planting

In the listing of ground covers (pages 56–95), certain planting methods are called for. Explanations of these planting methods follow. If you need additional information, see "Planting Techniques" in the *Sunset* book *Basic Gardening Illustrated*.

Ground covers in nursery flats. If you buy carpeting plants such as *Dichon-dra, Thymus serpyllum,* or *Cymbalaria aequitriloba* in flats, turn the flat over to remove the plants in one large piece, cut the contents like a sheet cake into 1½-inch squares, then plant the squares in a grid pattern. If plants have been grown in individual plastic cells, pop the plants out of the cells, pull off any "callus" of wadded roots, and plant them. Spacing depends on the individual plant and how quickly you want it to fill in. For more information on plant spacing, check the listing for your particular plant.

Ground covers from cuttings. Many ground covers can be grown from cuttings taken from established plants, usually in mid to late spring. Simply cut off a branch tip with at least three sets of leaves, insert the cut end several inches into prepared soil (don't bury any foliage), firm the soil around it, and water well. Roots will develop along the buried stem. Or you can place the cuttings into flats filled with sand or a similar rooting material. When these cuttings have formed a root system, remove them from the flat and plant them individually in prepared soil as you would plants purchased in flats.

Ground covers from divisions. If you have plants that spread by developing roots and top growth in clumps, you can dig up a mature clump and separate it into independently rooted

How to Plant Ground Covers from Nursery Containers

Step 1: Dig planting hole, fill with water, and let it drain away.

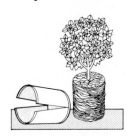

Step 2: Carefully remove plant from nursery container.

Step 3: Loosen roots with a sharp stick or knife; this helps plant adapt faster.

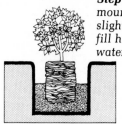

Step 4: Place plant on mound of soil so crown sits slightly above ground level; fill hole halfway with soil; water.

Step 5: Finish filling hole; create a watering basin; water plant.

sections. These new sections, called "divisions," can be planted in amended soil. If the sections don't pull apart easily, cut them apart with a sharp knife.

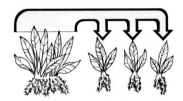

Ground covers from nursery containers. Most of the ground covers sold in nurseries come in gallon cans or plastic containers. When you purchase plants, choose those with a healthy, vigorous appearance and good foliage. Also, check the soil surface and the drainage holes for any sign of crowded roots; if any roots are visible, the plant is rootbound and transplanting may not be successful.

To plant a ground cover from a gallon can or larger container, dig a hole twice the size of the container. If you haven't already prepared the soil, you can mix amendments (see pages 6 and 8–9) into the soil you remove from the planting hole. Since many container plants grow in loose, light, fast-draining mixes that favor quick, even root development, their roots may not spread into denser, surrounding soil. You should also apply any nutrients the plants need to ensure proper growth.

Next, fill the planting hole with water and let it drain away completely (Step 1). Remove the plant from its container (Step 2), and loosen the roots with a sharp stick or knife (Step 3). Don't remove plants from their containers until you're ready to plant them; exposed roots can dry out rapidly.

Place the plant on a mound of soil so its crown sits slightly above ground level. Fill the hole about halfway up with the amended soil and water it in (Step 4). Finish filling the hole with amended soil, create a watering basin (see page 39), then water again (Step 5). Keep plants well watered until they are established; then follow the watering procedure recommended for your plants in the individual plant listing. If plants are in smaller containers (less than 1 gallon) or will be placed close together, just dig a hole and plant them.

Planting on a Slope

When part or all of your garden is located on a slope, you can use the hillside-hugging ground covers to your advantage. Ground covers, whether spreading or vining types, help to bind the soil, preventing soil erosion. They also provide a foliage cover for an otherwise bare or weedy slope. Some ground covers will even provide seasonal flowers or colorful foliage or berries. For a list of ground covers that thrive on hillsides, see page 54.

Planting Techniques

There are several ways to approach planting on a slope. Vining or spreading covers can be planted flush with the slope if it isn't too steep, then trained to grow either up or down. (Use bent wire shaped like croquet wickets to hold vines or upright branches in place.) You can terrace the entire slope. Or you can create an individual terrace for each plant; this technique is illustrated at top right. The individual terrace method permits you to improve the soil in the planting hole—if your ground covers need special soil—and to create a watering basin which keeps the individual plant watered and prevents excessive runoff.

Whichever planting method you use, water the plants well and mulch the entire area after planting. The mulch will help keep the soil moist and weed-free until the ground covers are established.

If your slope is steep, you may want to install a retaining wall to help hold the hill in place. One type of retaining wall is illustrated at lower right. For information on constructing retaining walls, see the Sunset books *Walks, Walls & Patio Floors* and *Garden & Patio Building Book*.

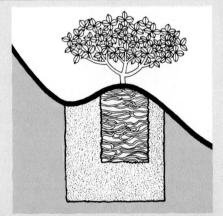

Creating individual terraces for plants on a slope lets you improve soil in planting hole and create a watering basin for plants that came in a gallon container or larger.

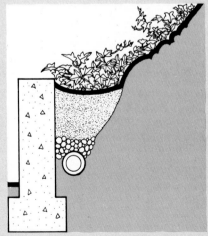

Retaining walls need adequate drainage; here drain tile diverts subsurface water. Vining ground covers can be placed at top of wall, trained to grow up slope.

Western Climate Zone Map

Many factors combine and interplay to establish plant climates. A plant climate is an area in which temperature ranges, humidity patterns, and geographic and seasonal characteristics combine to allow certain plants to succeed and others to fail.

The eight western plant climate zones are described below:

Zone A. The West's coldest winters. Snows every winter. Growing season varies from about 100 to 160 days, longer in favored areas.

Zone B. Puget Sound, Willamette Valley, Oregon and Washington coast. Ample rainfall, freezing winters, maritime influence.

Zone C. Mountains in southern Oregon, foothills in northern California. Hot dry summers, frosty winters, winter rainfall.

Zone D. Northern and central California interior valleys. Hot dry summers with occasional maritime influence. Rainy, frosty winters.

Zone E. Deserts, high to low. Amount of frost varies, but all share scant rainfall, low humidity, long hot summers.

Zone F. Coastal climate in southern Oregon, northern California, central California. Cool, often foggy summers. Cool wet winters with light frost.

Zone G. Southern California away from coast. Maritime influence varies, as does summer heat, amount and frequency of winter frost.

Zone H. Coastal and coast influences, southern California. Little or no frost, cooler summers, best area for tropicals.

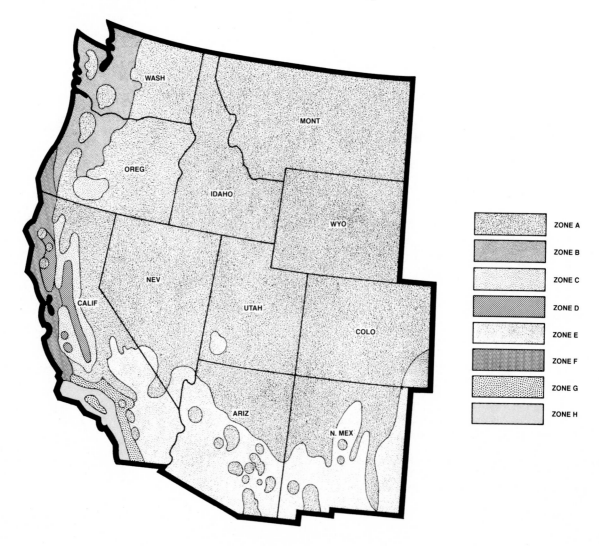

ZONE A
ZONE B
ZONE C
ZONE D
ZONE E
ZONE F
ZONE G
ZONE H

Eastern Climate Zone Map

The plant hardiness zone map below—devised by the United States Department of Agriculture—is used in countless nursery catalogs and garden books to indicate where plants can be grown. In the map's original concept, the reader was to locate on the map the climate zone in which he or she lived; then, if the zone number given for a particular plant was the same as, or smaller than, the reader's climate zone number, the plant was judged to be hardy in his or her locale and one that could be grown there with reasonable success.

In our listings, we have followed the standard method of hardiness rating, but with a difference—in addition to indicating the coldest zone in which the plant will grow, we consider its adaptability and usefulness in the warmer zones, and indicate all zones in which the plant is generally grown. The eastern climate zones are listed as numbers following the lettered western zones in the ground covers plant listing, pages 56–95.

The limitations of the map are obvious. It is impossible to accurately map local variations in climate. Furthermore, a map based only on temperatures is misleading when you're considering plants that have special requirements; for example, plants such as campanula, oxalis, or saxifraga prefer acid soils, but this soil will not necessarily be found throughout their range of favorable growing climates. In our listings we point out this type of localization within zones by noting all plants that require acid soil, as well as any other special needs the ground covers might have.

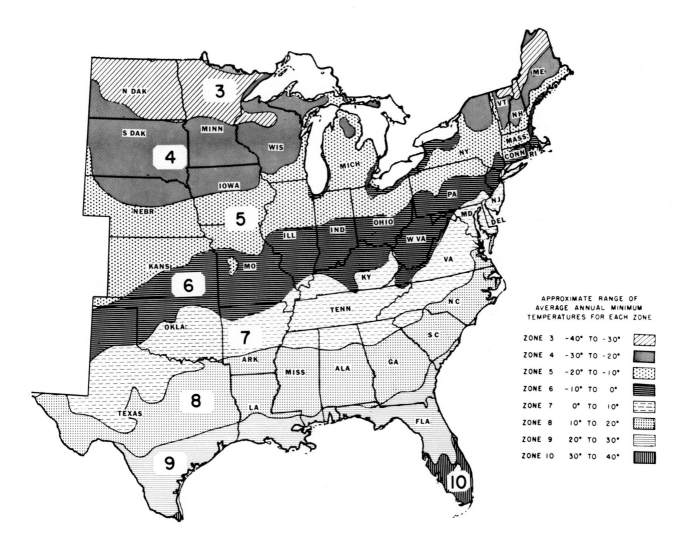

APPROXIMATE RANGE OF
AVERAGE ANNUAL MINIMUM
TEMPERATURES FOR EACH ZONE

ZONE 3   -40° TO -30°
ZONE 4   -30° TO -20°
ZONE 5   -20° TO -10°
ZONE 6   -10° TO   0°
ZONE 7   0° TO 10°
ZONE 8   10° TO 20°
ZONE 9   20° TO 30°
ZONE 10 30° TO 40°

Ground Covers: Versatile Problem Solver.

Included in the group we commonly label "ground covers" are plants so numerous, so varied, and so able to thrive in or adapt to many different climates and landscape situations that to describe them as "versatile" is almost an understatement. There are ground covers to fit any landscape need—ground-hugging lawn substitutes that you can walk on, plants to splash or sprinkle color over large areas with their seasonal displays of flower or foliage, plants that can adapt to less-than-perfect growing situations such as hot sun, poor or dry soil, or deep shade. There are hard-working ground covers to control erosion on steep slopes, and ground covers that can take neglect. Whatever your needs, the ground covers can probably meet them.

The comprehensive plant listing on pages 56–95 includes plants that are naturally low-growing or spreading. Most plants listed will stay under 3 feet in height; others can serve as barrier plants or can be pruned or trimmed to stay low.

In this section, we deal with several common landscape problems and the ground covers that can solve them.

The lawn substitutes. These carpeting ground covers stay close to the ground, giving the uniformity of a grass lawn but with a different color or texture. Some provide seasonal flowers, and a few can withstand foot traffic.

Some gardeners turn to the lawn substitutes to avoid the constant upkeep a well-groomed lawn requires; others may turn to these ground covers because of cultural problems such as acid or moist soil, or deep shade.

The colorful ground covers. Here, ground covers serve two purposes: they solve landscape problems and provide a splash of color. Some covers, such as ice plant, erica, or osteospermum give one large flower display; others bloom over a long period of time; a few offer colorful fall foliage or berries.

Ground covers for hillsides. Hillside landscapes can present many problems—erosion, inadequate drainage, poor soil—that selected ground covers can handle. These plants provide strong root systems that prevent erosion on unstable slopes and help eliminate weed problems. And certain covers thrive in dry or poor soils.

Shade-loving ground covers. Plants in shady spots must adapt to lower levels of light intensity and a cooler atmosphere than plants in nearby sunny areas. You'll find many ground covers that actually prefer these shady glens.

Drought-tolerant ground covers. Whether your drought problem is constant or just occasional, you'll want to find plants that will grow with little or no water. Some ground covers adapt quickly to drought situations; others will need to become established before they can fend for themselves.

Natural rocks and pebbles. These, of course, aren't plants at all, but they are included in this section because they can solve many of the same problems that ground cover plants can—helping eliminate weeds, keeping the soil covered, and providing interesting colors and textures. They can be used in any garden situation, and they need only minimal maintenance.

If It's Color You Want...

For many gardeners, a successful landscape is one that contains seasonal color displays. If you agree, use these lists of ground covers arranged by the seasons in which they bloom. The page reference following each plant name indicates the location of the individual plant description. For more ideas on using colorful ground covers, see "Cover the Ground with Splashes of Color" on pages 46–47.

Spring

Arctotheca, page 57
Armeria, page 57
Bergenia, page 58
Ceanothus, page 59
Cistus, page 60
Coreopsis, page 60
Cornus, page 60
Fragaria, page 71
Galium, page 71
Gazania, page 72
Helianthemum, page 73
Hemerocallis, page 73
Iberis, page 74
Ice plant, pages 74, 79
Jasminum, page 79
Osteospermum, page 82
Phlox, page 82
Phyla, page 82

Potentilla, page 87
Ranunculus, page 87
Rosa, pages 87–88
Rosmarinus, page 88
Sedum, page 89
Thymus, pages 89–90
Tiarella, page 90
Veronica, pages 90, 95
Vinca, page 95

Summer

Achillea, page 56
Arctotheca, page 57
Bougainvillea, page 58
Campanula, page 59
Convolvulus, page 60
Coreopsis, page 60
Dianthus, page 66
Duchesnea, page 66
Erica, page 66

Erigeron, pages 66, 71
Gardenia, pages 71–72
Gazania, page 72
Geranium, page 72
Hebe, page 73
Hypericum, page 74
Ice plant, pages 74, 79
Lantana, page 79
Lonicera, page 80
Myosotis, page 81
Nepeta, page 81
Nierembergia, page 81
Pelargonium, page 82
Phyla, page 82
Potentilla, page 87
Rosa, pages 87–88
Santolina, page 88
Teucrium, page 89
Trachelospermum, page 90
Verbena, page 90
Zauschneria, page 95

Fall

Convolvulus, page 60
Coreopsis, page 60
Dianthus, page 66
Erica, page 66
Erigeron, pages 66, 71
Hemerocallis, page 73
Osteospermum, page 82
Phyla, page 82
Vinca, page 95

Winter

Bergenia, page 58
Iberis, page 74
Ice plant, page 74, 79
Jasminum, page 79
Osteospermum, page 82
Pyracantha (berries), page 87
Rosmarinus, page 88

These Covers Form a Carpet

If you don't need a conventional lawn to walk or play on, but you still want the same landscape effect, consider the carpeting ground covers. These ground-hugging plants offer the same neatness and uniformity as a grass lawn, without the need for frequent maintenance. They come in an array of foliage textures and colors. Some provide a bonus of seasonal flowers. And a few of these living carpets will even withstand occasional foot traffic.

If you buy carpeting plants in flats, cut the contents like a sheet cake into 1½-inch squares, then plant the squares (see page 37). If you buy plants in plastic cells, just pop them out of the cells and plant them. Spacing for the squares is given under each individual plant listing on pages 56–95. Close spacing will cost more, but it will give fast coverage.

Besides the seven carpeting ground covers shown, additional low growers to consider are listed on page 54, under "Good Lawn Substitutes."

Shade-loving **Soleirolia soleirolii** *forms a thick, lush cover between broken concrete pads. Known as baby's tears (see description on page 89), it requires protection from hot summer sun, frequent waterings to keep ground moist. Used as cover, soleirolia rarely needs to be trimmed.*

Comparison of six flats of carpeting ground covers shows differences in color, texture, leaf shapes. These covers include, upper left, Cymbalaria aequitriloba (see page 65); upper right, Pratia angulata (see page 87); center left, Viola hederacea (see page 95); center right, Laurentia fluviatilis (see page 80); lower left, Thymus (see pages 89–90); lower right, Cymbalaria muralis (see page 65).

Ground covers with bluish purple flowers form foundation of this colorful landscape. Nierembergia 'Purple Robe' (see page 81) is below wall, Convolvulus (see page 60) is on top of wall. Together they serve as permanent foils for rotating annuals.

Colorful ground covers combine to create interesting landscape. Covers in foreground are yellow-flowered helianthemum (see page 73) and Origanum dictamnus (see page 82). Others include Nepeta faassenii (see page 81) and Veronica prostrata (see pages 90, 95).

Easy-to-care-for landscape features several prostrate junipers (see page 79), plus Vinca minor in foreground, Trachelospermum jasminoides along house wall. Vinca (see description on page 95) and star jasmine (see page 90) provide summer flowers. These covers need infrequent watering, trimming.

Cover the Ground with Splashes of Color

Most people think of ground covers as hard-working landscape problem solvers—plants that will grow on steep hillsides, thrive in shady areas, serve as low-growing fillers between trees and shrubs, even replace time-consuming lawns. But a solution to your landscape problem isn't the only thing you can expect of ground covers—with careful selection you can use these same plants to create an unexpected show of color.

Restraint should be your byword, though, when you plan your colorful landscape. Avoid combining too many colors, or colors that will clash. The safest approach is to build around already existing landscape features, such as permanent trees and shrubs that bloom or have interesting foliage, or the exterior color of your house, fence, or other structures.

Many of the ground covers listed in the plant encyclopedia (pages 56–95) provide seasonal flowers; others have interesting foliage colors or fruit to offer. On page 44, the colorful ground covers are listed by seasons.

Here are three good ways to use colorful ground covers in your landscape:
• mix several different ground covers that have flower colors
• use one or two covers in similar colors as permanent plantings that will serve as foils for a rotating display of annual plants
• use a large planting of a single flowering ground cover for one sensational color splash

Sunshine yellow flowers of Sunburst coreopsis (see page 60) in foreground and pale yellow clusters of achillea (see page 56) at right center mix with other perennials for summer border.

Mass plantings of Polygonum capitatum, Juniperus conferta create low-maintenance entry garden. Pink flowers of polygonum (see description on page 87) complement evergreen shore juniper (see description on page 79).

Ground Covers for Hillside Landscapes

Ground covers and hillsides just naturally go together. Once established as hillside plantings, ground covers provide strong root systems that control erosion on unstable slopes, help eliminate most weed problems, require little maintenance (if chosen carefully), and create a pleasing landscape on an otherwise barren slope.

The ground covers shown on these two pages offer interesting foliage and colorful flowers for hillside plantings. Other low-growing plants that perform well on slopes are listed on page 54, under "For Hillsides, Erosion Control."

Since hillsides tend to offer less than ideal growing conditions for plants, you should select ground covers that will cope—some grow well in poor or shallow soil; others can tolerate wind or hot sun. And because plants on slopes are also difficult to water, you should either select ground covers that require little water or plan to form a watering basin (see page 39) around each plant so water will soak in rather than run down the slope.

Spreading or mounding perennials commonly known as rock garden plants or alpines make a colorful ground cover planting for a well-drained hillside, gentle slope, or mounds. Too numerous to name, the covers planted here provide a year-round color display while suppressing weeds. For kinds available in your area, check local nurseries that specialize in perennials or rock garden plants.

Hillside tapestry of several different ericas (see description on page 66) creates a colorful planting in spring, summer. When plants are out of bloom, tapestry effect continues in shades of green. Heathers thrive in cool-summer areas.

Spectacular color display on this terraced hillside comes mainly from different forms of ice plant (see descriptions on pages 74, 79) and pelargoniums (see descriptions on page 82). Both plants are sun-loving, need only infrequent waterings.

Shade-loving Ground Covers

Shaded areas—the province especially of established gardens—offer a lower level of light intensity and a cooler atmosphere than nearby sunny locations. Whether your shady spot is caused by large, mature trees or shrubs or by nearby houses or other structures that obscure light, you can find a number of ground covers that will thrive.

Frequently people fall into the trap of trying to grow sun-loving plants in their shaded gardens. These misplaced plants lose their vibrant foliage color, grow spindly and lanky, and refuse to bloom.

The ground covers shown here, as well as those listed under "Partial to Full Shade" on pages 54–55, actually prefer a shaded garden. They thrive in the cooler, moist climate, and some even produce flowers in the lower light levels. In short, they are shade-loving ground covers.

Good under large trees, vaccinium and vancouveria create natural woodland ground cover. Vaccinium vitis-idaea and Vancouveria planipetala (see page 90 for both) are grown for interesting foliage.

Shade lovers include erica (see page 66), Cotoneaster horizontalis (page 65), lysimachia (page 80).

Contrasting greens of liriope (see page 80), soleirolia (see page 89) make lush, thick cover.

Surrounded by trees, house, this corner of garden gets early morning sun followed by deep shade. Adaptable ground covers include Hedera helix (see page 73), hostas (see pages 73–74), erica (see page 66). Design: R. David Adams.

The Drought-tolerant Ground Covers

Some gardeners must deal with the problem of drought. Many areas—much of the West, for example—are characterized by a short annual rainy season followed by months in which gardens receive no natural moisture. Other areas face periodically recurring drought years in which rainfall levels are far below normal and water use for landscape irrigation may be restricted or costly. If yours is a drought-prone area, consider planting a drought-tolerant ground cover.

Once established, the plants shown on this page—as well as the other plants listed under "Drought Tolerant" on page 54—will thrive with little or no water during the normal dry season. To become drought tolerant, these covers need to send roots down to a soil level where some moisture from winter rain will remain far into the dry season.

To help newly planted drought-tolerant ground covers adjust, plant them in early fall to take advantage of the winter rain. If rains aren't frequent, you should water drought-tolerant plants during their first winter and spring, enough to keep the soil damp. Then, during their first dry season, water them deeply three or four times. By their second summer, most of these covers should be on their own, able to manage without irrigation.

Pair of low growers gives best display for least water. Santolina (see page 88) has yellow flowers all summer; Rosmarinus officinalis (see page 88) produces blue flowers in winter.

Summer-blooming Coreopsis verticillata (see page 60) needs no summer water once it's established.

Pink-flowered Teucrium chamaedrys (see page 89) blooms all summer in hot, dry spots.

Billowy bed of Baccharis pilularis (see page 58) serves as evergreen background for colorful perennials. Design: Lester Hawkins.

A SAMPLING OF ROCKS AND PEBBLES

Rounded stone

1. Black Mexican pebbles, 1 by 2 and 3 by 5-inch sizes. Smooth, flat beach pebbles imported from Mexico.

2. Quartz pebbles, 2 by 4 inches. Popular black and white river rock.

3. Large cobbles, 3 by 8 inches. Chunky, well-rounded stone with rustic good looks.

5. Medium cobbles, 2 by 4 inches. Smaller version of number 3.

7. Red Mexican pebbles (Rosaritos), ½ by 1 inch. A red-tinged, smaller variety of number 1.

8. San Pedro pebbles, 1½ inches. Attractive solid color is "flat" or nonreflective.

12. Lomita stone (Palos Verdes pebbles), 1½ inches. Ocean pebbles unusual for their blond highlights.

13. Red river aggregates (red beach pebbles), ½ inch. Popular for smooth texture and subtle coloring.

15. Quartz pebbles, ¼ inch. Smaller form of number 2.

17. Pea gravel, ¼ inch. Widely available loose aggregate in small sizes.

Crushed rock

4. Taffy (Sonoma rose, ginger rock), 1½ inches. Chalky surface, unusual coloration are eye-catching.

6. Brown rock, ½ inch. Flinty, hard edged. Reddish mahogany tones complement redwood, dark woods.

9. Cinder rock (lava rock, scoria), ⅜ inch. Common rock in the West. Brittle and lightweight; not very durable.

14. Brown gravel, ¾ inch. Inexpensive and versatile.

16. Gold rock (Pacific gold, desert gold), ⅜ inch. Mica, quartz highlights give this granite its name.

Fine-textured materials

10. Gold dust. Granular form of gold rock, number 16; soft, sunny color.

11. Mocha fines. Decomposed brown gravel, number 14. Rich earth tones naturalize well.

18. Olympia sand. Clean, light color with a fairly coarse texture.

19. Green fines. Also called "crusher run base" at rock yards.

Natural Rock
—for an Almost-maintenance-free
Ground Cover

Many gardeners find that natural rock can be a problem-solving ground cover. Rock materials fall into three categories—round, crushed, and fine-textured—and are available in a pleasing assortment of colors and sizes.

Gravel and loose aggregates have a number of garden uses. They make practical and inexpensive "soft" paving materials. They can be used as a mulch or for covering awkward spots where plants won't grow. And they can cover areas that haven't been landscaped yet; then when time, money, or weather conditions are right, you just push the rocks aside and plant your trees or shrubs.

Visually, natural rock combines well with plants, structures, and other surfaces in a garden's design. Dyed rock in bright, eye-catching colors may be harder to live with.

When you're choosing rock at a rock yard, keep in mind that colors will become more intense over a large area, and that sun or shade will affect them. Also, consider whether or not leaves or other garden debris will be a problem. For a rakeable ground cover, choose small rock materials— ½ inch or less in diameter.

To find rock suppliers, check the Yellow Pages under "Building Supplies," "Garden Supplies," or "Rock & Stone." Ask for gravel, loose aggregates, or decorative rock. Some garden centers may offer these materials prepackaged, but you'll find the best selection in a large supply yard.

Names of rock materials will vary from place to place, so buy rock by appearance to be sure you get the color and size you want. Also, keep in mind that local rock materials should be less expensive than imports.

Types of Rock

In addition to color and size, rock materials are divided according to shape and texture. The type of rock you choose will determine the overall appearance of the finished ground cover and the area's uses.

Round stones have been naturally smoothed by the action of glaciers, streams, or the ocean. Also labeled "water-washed pebbles" or "river rock," they range from ⅛ to ¼ inch in diameter (pea gravel) all the way to 8 inches across (cobbles). The small sizes make good walking surfaces, though they may roll underfoot. To prevent this, you can pack them down or get a mix of sizes that will fit together tightly; a ¾-inch mix containing rocks from ½ to 1½ inch wide is good. Cobbles

can be set into the ground or used decoratively in areas away from paths.

Crushed rock is sharp-edged gravel made from larger quarried rock in sizes from ¼ to 1½ inches. It is often sold as "decorative stone" and comes in both dyed and natural colors. The natural tones—rust, tan, brown, and gray—are most useful. White and bright colors reflect hot sun and may be difficult to keep clean. Use the ½-inch size for walkways, larger sizes for ground covers.

Fine-textured materials are pulverized forms of crushed rock in such colors as tan, brown, gray, dark red, and black. They make attractive paths, driveways, terraces, and game courts, since they pack easily into a dense, smooth surface that wears well and can be raked.

Coverage and Installation

In most instances, smooth and crushed rocks are spread in 2 to 3-inch layers, fine-textured materials in 2 to 4-inch layers. Actual coverage will depend on the size and weight of the material, but generally a ton of medium-size rock covers 100 square feet to a depth of 2 inches. Cost varies considerably, depending on the type of rock you choose, the amount you need, and any delivery charges.

Laying a rock ground cover usually requires only minimal site preparation. Plan to grade the soil as you would for a lawn (see pages 8–9) and install any permanent edging beforehand; a good guide is the Sunset book *How to Build Walks, Walls & Patio Floors.*

To control weeds, you can lay plastic sheeting before the rock layer goes down; otherwise, use a chemical weed killer such as a pre-emergent herbicide, or plan to pull the weeds out by hand as they appear. Haul the rocks to the site, then just rake and smooth them into place.

For compacted surfaces like paths and driveways, you'll need a roller and some time and energy. Apply the rock in 1-inch layers, wetting each layer and rolling it thoroughly.

Maintenance

Most rock ground covers need only occasional raking and weeding. Heavy-use surfaces will need to be renewed every few years with the addition of new rocks.

Ground Covers for Specific Situations

You may find that your landscape contains some challenging spots—a steep hillside, an area in constant shade, a place with poor or dry soil—that limit your choices of ground covers. On these two pages, we list common landscape problems and the ground covers that will adapt to these conditions, and even thrive. Following each plant name is a page reference, indicating the location of the individual plant description.

For Hillsides, Erosion Control

Arctostaphylos, pages 56–57
Arctotheca, page 57
Arundinaria, page 57
Asparagus, page 57
Atriplex, page 58
Bougainvillea, page 58
Ceanothus, page 59
Cissus, page 60
Cistus, page 60
Convolvulus, page 60
Coprosma, page 60
Coronilla, page 60
Correa, pages 60, 65
Cotoneaster, page 65
Gazania, page 72
Hippocrepis, page 73
Ice plant, pages 74, 79
Lathyrus, page 80
Lonicera, page 80
Osteospermum, page 82
Parthenocissus, page 82
Pelargonium, page 82
Polygonum, page 87
Rosa, pages 87–88
Zauschneria, page 95

Drought Tolerant

(Able to endure extended periods without irrigation once established)
Achillea, page 56
Arabis, page 56
Arctostaphylos, pages 56–57
Arctotheca, page 57
Asparagus, page 57
Atriplex, page 58
Baccharis, page 58
Ceanothus, page 59
Cerastium, page 59
Cistus, page 60
Convolvulus, page 60
Coprosma, page 60
Cytisus, page 65
Erigeron, pages 66, 71
Gelsemium, page 72
Grevillea, pages 72–73
Ice plant, pages 74, 79
Lonicera, page 80
Mahonia, pages 80–81
Mentha, page 81
Myoporum, page 81
Origanum, page 82
Osteospermum, page 82
Ribes, page 87
Rosmarinus, page 88
Verbena, page 90

Will Take Light Foot Traffic

Arenaria, page 57
Chamaemelum, page 59
Duchesnea, page 66
Erodium, page 71
Fragaria, page 71
Glechoma, page 72
Herniaria, page 73
Hippocrepis, page 73
Laurentia, page 80
Lotus corniculatus, page 80
Mazus, page 81
Mentha, page 81
Muehlenbeckia, page 81
Nepeta, page 81
Phyla, page 82
Potentilla, page 87
Sagina, page 88
Satureja, page 88
Soleirolia, page 89
Vinca, page 95

For Small Spaces

Achillea, page 56
Agapanthus, page 56
Arabis, page 56
Arenaria, page 57
Armeria, page 57
Bellis, page 58
Campanula, page 59
Cerastium, page 59
Convallaria, page 60
Cornus, page 60
Cytisus, page 65
Dianthus, page 66
Epimedium, page 66
Erodium, page 71
Festuca, page 71
Galax, page 71
Galium, page 71
Gardenia, page 71–72
Gaultheria, page 72
Genista, page 72
Geranium, page 72
Glechoma, page 72

Hebe, page 73
Helianthemum, page 73
Hemerocallis, page 73
Hosta, pages 73–74
Liriope, page 80
Myosotis, page 81
Origanum, page 82
Pelargonium, page 82
Rosmarinus, page 88
Ruscus, page 88
Sagina, page 88
Santolina, page 88
Satureja, page 88
Saxifraga, page 88
Sedum, page 89
Teucrium, page 89
Thymus, pages 89–90
Trachelospermum, page 90
Vaccinium, page 90
Vancouveria, page 90
Veronica, pages 90, 95
Vinca, page 95
Viola, page 95
Zauschneria, page 95
Zoysia, page 95

Good Lawn Substitutes

Arenaria, page 57
Chamaemelum, page 59
Cymbalaria, page 65
Duchesnea, page 66
Fragaria, page 71
Glechoma, page 72
Herniaria, page 73
Hippocrepis, page 73
Laurentia, page 80
Lotus corniculatus, page 80
Mazus, page 81
Nepeta, page 81
Phyla, page 82
Potentilla, page 87
Pratia, page 87
Soleirolia, page 89

Partial to Full Shade

Aegopodium, page 56
Arenaria, page 57
Asarum, page 57
Bergenia, page 58
Convallaria, page 60
Cornus, page 60
Cymbalaria, page 65
Duchesnea, page 66
Epimedium, page 66
Euonymus, page 71
Fatshedera, page 71
Galax, page 71
Galium, page 71
Gaultheria, page 72
Glechoma, page 72
Hedera, page 73
Herniaria, page 73
Hosta, pages 73–74
Hypericum, page 74
Laurentia, page 80
Lysimachia, page 80
Mahonia, pages 80–81

Myosotis, page 81
Nepeta, page 81
Oxalis, page 82
Pachysandra, page 82
Ranunculus, page 87
Ruscus, page 88
Sarcococca, page 88
Satureja, page 88
Saxifraga, page 88
Soleirolia, page 89
Symphoricarpos, page 89
Tiarella, page 90
Tolmiea, page 90
Tradescantia, page 90
Vancouveria, page 90
Viburnum, page 95
Vinca, page 95
Viola, page 95
Xanthorhiza, page 95

Like Moist or Acid Soil

Asarum, page 57
Calluna, page 58
Campanula, page 59
Convallaria, page 60
Cornus, page 60
Epimedium, page 66
Erica, page 66
Euonymus, page 71
Galax, page 71
Galium, page 71
Gaultheria, page 72
Lysimachia, page 80
Myosotis, page 81
Oxalis, page 82
Pachysandra, page 82
Paxistima, page 82
Ranunculus, page 87
Satureja, page 88
Saxifraga, page 88
Tiarella, page 90
Tolmiea, page 90
Tradescantia, page 90
Vaccinium, page 90
Viburnum, page 95
Viola, page 95
Xanthorhiza, page 95

For Large Areas

Aegopodium, page 56
Ajuga, page 56
Arctostaphylos, pages 56–57
Arctotheca, page 57
Asarum, page 57
Asparagus, page 57
Atriplex, page 58
Ceanothus, page 59
Ceratostigma, page 59
Chamaemelum, page 59
Cistus, page 60
Coprosma, page 60
Coronilla, page 60
Cotoneaster, page 65
Duchesnea, page 66
Erica, page 66
Euonymus, page 71
Fatshedera, page 71
Ficus, page 71
Gazania, page 72

Grevillea, pages 72–73
Hedera, page 73
Hemerocallis, page 73
Hypericum, page 74
Jasminum, page 79
Juniperus, page 79
Lantana, page 79
Lonicera, page 80
Myoporum, page 81
Osteospermum, page 82
Parthenocissus, page 82
Pelargonium, page 82
Ranunculus, page 87
Ribes, page 87
Rosa, pages 87–88
Rosmarinus, page 88
Teucrium, page 89
Trachelospermum, page 90
Vinca, page 95
Xanthorhiza, page 95

Full Sun to Light Shade

Achillea, page 56
Agapanthus, page 56
Ajuga, page 56
Arabis, page 56
Arctostaphylos, pages 56–57
Arctotheca, page 57
Armeria, page 57
Arundinaria, page 57
Asparagus, page 57
Atriplex, page 58
Baccharis, page 58
Bougainvillea, page 58
Campanula, page 59
Ceanothus, page 59
Cerastium, page 59
Ceratostigma, page 59
Chamaemelum, page 59
Cistus, page 60
Convolvulus, page 60
Coprosma, page 60
Coreopsis, page 60
Coronilla, page 60
Correa, pages 60, 65
Cotoneaster, page 65
Cotula, page 65
Cytisus, page 65
Dianthus, page 66
Duchesnea, page 66
Erigeron, pages 66, 71
Erodium, page 71
Euonymus, page 71
Festuca, page 71
Ficus, page 71
Fragaria, page 71
Gazania, page 72
Gelsemium, page 72
Genista, page 72
Geranium, page 72
Grevillea, pages 72–73
Hedera, page 73
Helianthemum, page 73
Hemerocallis, page 73
Herniaria, page 73
Hippocrepis, page 73
Hypericum, page 74
Iberis, page 74
Ice plant, pages 74, 79

Jasminum, page 79
Juniperus, page 79
Lantana, page 79
Lathyrus, page 80
Liriope, page 80
Lonicera, page 80
Lotus, page 80
Mahonia, pages 80–81
Mazus, page 81
Mentha, page 81
Muehlenbeckia, page 81
Myoporum, page 81
Nepeta, page 81
Nierembergia, page 81
Ophiopogon, page 81
Origanum, page 82
Osteospermum, page 82
Parthenocissus, page 82
Paxistima, page 82
Pelargonium, page 82
Phlox, page 82
Phyla, page 82
Polygonum, page 87
Potentilla, page 87
Pratia, page 87
Pyracantha, page 87
Ribes, page 87
Rosa, pages 87–88
Rosmarinus, page 88
Sagina, page 88
Santolina, page 88
Sedum, page 89
Teucrium, page 89
Thymus, pages 89–90
Trachelospermum, page 90
Vaccinium, page 90
Verbena, page 90
Veronica, pages 90, 95
Xanthorhiza, page 95
Zauschneria, page 95
Zoysia, page 95

Tolerate Dry or Poor Soil

(Able to thrive with casual care in rocky, sandy, or infertile soil; or where roots of trees or larger shrubs steal most of water)

Aegopodium, page 56
Arctotheca, page 57
Asparagus, page 57
Atriplex, page 58
Carissa, page 59
Ceratostigma, page 59
Coprosma, page 60
Correa, pages 60, 65
Cytisus, page 65
Gazania, page 72
Grevillea, pages 72–73
Hemerocallis, page 73
Hypericum, page 74
Juniperus, page 79
Lantana, page 79
Lonicera, page 80
Origanum, page 82
Rosmarinus, page 88
Teucrium, page 89
Thymus, pages 89–90
Zauschneria, page 95

Ground Covers ... from A to Z

This comprehensive guide offers you a list of plants that make good ground covers. Each listing includes a description of the plant's appearance and growth habits, its care requirements, and any other related varieties that can also serve as gound covers.

Many of these ground covers are pictured to help you locate and identify them. Most of the plants listed can be found as seed or in flats or various sized containers in nurseries, garden centers, or specialty nurseries.

Plants are listed alphabetically by their botanical names. Common name listings will direct you to the botanical name listing. To find your correct climate zone, see the climate zone maps on pages 42 and 43. The "lettered" zones (Zones A–H) cover the western United States, and the "numbered" zones (Zones 3–10) cover the eastern United States.

Aaron's beard. See Hypericum

ACHILLEA. Yarrow. Perennial. Yarrows thrive in sun, require only routine care. Moderate watering in dry climates, but can withstand drought when established. Gray or green ferny, scented foliage; flat clusters of flowers in summer; shear after flowers fade to prolong bloom. Divide when clumps get crowded. See photos on pages 47, 61.

A. ageratifolia. Greek yarrow. *Culture:* Zones A–H, 4–10; full sun; no foot traffic; best in small areas; fast growing. Set nursery plants 6–12 inches apart. *Foliage and flowers:* Mats of silvery leaves, nearly smooth edged to somewhat lobed. In summer and fall, white flat flower clusters appear on stems from 4–10 inches tall.

A. clavennae (*A. argentea*). Silvery yarrow. *Culture:* Same as *A. ageratifolia. Foliage and flowers:* Mats of silvery gray, chrysanthemumlike, lobed leaves. In summer and fall, ivory white flat flower clusters, about 3/4 inch across, grow on stems from 5–10 inches tall.

A. tomentosa. Woolly yarrow. Most common yarrow in nurseries. *Culture:* Same as *A. ageratifolia.* Will tolerate light shade. *Foliage and flowers:* Ferny, hairy leaves spread to form a flat, deep green mat. Golden yellow flat flower clusters bloom in summer on stems 6–10 inches tall. 'Primrose Beauty' has pale yellow flowers.

AEGOPODIUM. Bishop's weed, gout-weed. Deciduous perennial. Common in cold climates; nurseries rarely sell plants, so try to obtain divisions from friends or neighbors. Creeping underground runners can be invasive; confine plants within a buried barrier of wood or concrete. Keep plants low and even by mowing 2 or 3 times during growing season.

A. podagraria 'Variegatum'. Variegated Bishop's weed. Most common form of plant. *Culture:* Zones A–C, 4–8; light to full shade; no heavy foot traffic; good for large areas; fast growing in any type soil. Set divisions about 12 inches apart. *Foliage and flowers:* Many light green, divided leaves with white edges form a mass up to 6 inches high. Each leaflet can reach 3 inches long. Foliage dies to the ground in winter, sprouts again in spring. Summer flowers insignificant.

AGAPANTHUS 'Peter Pan'. Dwarf lily-of-the-Nile. Evergreen perennial with thick rootstocks and fleshy roots; dwarf form of plant. *Culture:* Zones C–D, E (warmest parts), F–H, 9–10; full sun to light shade; no foot traffic; best in small areas; fast growing. Set divisions of roots or nursery plants about 12 inches apart; divide plants if they become overcrowded. *Foliage and flowers:* Clumps of strap-shaped leaves 8–12 inches tall; clumps gradually grow wider as new plants form at edges. Long stalks up to 18 inches tall bear loose globes of blue flowers in summer. Larger, standard plants good for borders, edgings. See photo on page 61.

AJUGA reptans. Carpet bugle. Perennial. Extremely popular ground cover that comes in many sizes and leaf colors. Names of varieties listed

below may differ in nursery trade. Plants spread by runners, divide easily. *Culture:* Zones A–H, 4–10; sun or light shade; no foot traffic; for large or small areas; fast growing; well-drained soil; regular watering. Subject to root-knot nematodes. Set out plants or divisions 6–12 inches apart for standard-size plants, 18 inches apart for giants. *Foliage and flowers:* Dark green, lustrous leaves 2–3 inches long form a low dense cover that grows 2–3 inches wide in full sun, 3–4 inches wide in light shade. Blue to faintly purplish flowers in spring, early summer on 6–9-inch stiff spikes that should be sheared or mowed after bloom. Varieties include 'Burgundy Lace', reddish purple foliage variegated white and pink; 'Giant Bronze'; 'Giant Green'; 'Jungle Bronze', wavy-edged leaves, 10-inch flower spikes; 'Jungle Green', mounding growth, largest leaves; 'Purpurea' or 'Atropurpurea', bronze to purplish leaves; 'Variegata', leaves edged and splotched with yellow. See photo on page 61.

Algerian ivy. See Hedera

Allegheny foam flower. See Tiarella

Amaracus. See Origanum

Anthemis. See Chamaemelum nobile

ARABIS caucasica (*A. albida*). Wall rockcress. Perennial. Native Mediterranean ground cover good over spring bulb plantings. *Culture:* Zones A–H, 6–9; sun or light shade in hot climates; no foot traffic; best in small areas; moderate growth; withstands drought. In spring or fall, set out cuttings or nursery plants 8 inches apart, or sow seeds in prepared soil. Short-lived in warm-winter areas. *Foliage and flowers:* Mats of gray leaves grow to 6 inches high. *A.c.* 'Variegata' leaves have creamy white margins. Half-inch flowers in white or pinks cover plant in spring. Shear flowers and stems after bloom to maintain neatness.

ARCTOSTAPHYLOS. Manzanita. Evergreen western native shrubs with leathery, usually glossy foliage, handsome reddish bark, and clusters of bell-like flowers. None take foot traffic.

Climate Zone Maps, pages 42–43

Most grow rather slowly, with branches rooting as they touch the ground; mulch with peat moss, sawdust, fir bark to control weeds. Keep soil moist to encourage rooting of branches. See photos on page 62.

A. densiflora. Vine Hill manzanita. *Culture:* Zones C, D, F, G, may not be successful east of the Rockies; full sun; no foot traffic; good in large areas; slow growing; withstands drought. Does best on northeast or east slopes with good drainage, loose soil. Set nursery plants 3–5 feet apart. *Foliage and flowers:* Small glossy leaves are light to dark green, depending on variety. Bark is smooth, reddish black. Branches root where they touch the ground. White to pinkish bell-shaped flowers in late winter to early spring. 'Howard McMinn' forms mounds to 30 inches tall, up to 7 feet across in 5 years; pinch or prune any vertical branches to keep growth low, dense. 'James West', lower-growing form.

A. edmundsii. Little Sur manzanita. *Culture:* Zones C, D, F–H, may not be successful east of the Rockies; full shade to full sun; no foot traffic; good in large areas; slow growing; withstands drought. Set nursery plants 3–6 feet apart. Will grow in heavy soils. If drainage is slow, plant on slight mound so base of plant will not remain waterlogged. *Foliage and flowers:* Roundish, light green, 1-inch leaves on reddish stems. Plants grow from 4–24 inches tall, can spread more than 12 feet. Pinkish flowers in early winter.

A. hookeri 'Monterey Carpet'. Monterey manzanita. *Culture:* Zones C, D, F–H, may not be successful east of the Rockies; full sun; no foot traffic; good in large areas; slow growing; withstands drought. Set nursery plants 3–5 feet apart. *Foliage and flowers:* Bright green, glossy, 3/4-inch leaves on stems with red brown bark. Plants spread slowly to 12 feet across, 1 foot high. White to pinkish flowers in winter and spring, followed by clusters of bright red berries.

A. media. Zones B–D, F–H, may not be successful east of the Rockies. Like *A. uva-ursi* but taller, reaching up to 2 feet. Spreads more quickly.

A. pumila. Dune manzanita. *Culture:* Zones F–H, may not be successful east of the Rockies; full sun; no foot traffic; good in large areas; slow growing; withstands drought; needs sandy or well-drained soil. Set nursery plants 3–5 feet apart. *Foliage and flowers:* Narrowish, dull green leaves to 1 inch long on branches that root freely where they touch ground. Grows

to 2½ feet tall. Short dense clusters of small white to pink flowers in winter.

A. uva-ursi. Bearberry, Kinnikinnick. Most common ground cover manzanita. *Culture:* Zones A–D, F–H, 3–7; full sun; no foot traffic; good in large areas; slow to start; withstands drought. Set nursery plants 3–6 feet apart; mulch heavily with peat moss or composted sawdust to keep weeds out. *Foliage and flowers:* Prostrate plants spread to 15 feet across, rooting along branches. Bright glossy green, leathery leaves turn red in winter. White to pink flowers, followed by red or pink berries. 'Point Reyes' has dark green, closely set leaves. 'Radiant' has light green leaves, more widely spaced; produces heavy crops of bright red berries that last into winter.

ARCTOTHECA calendula. Cape weed. Evergreen perennial. Excellent for large areas that are difficult to care for. Requires a mild climate. Grows along freeways in California. *Culture:* Zones D, F–H, 9–10; full sun; best with no foot traffic; good for slopes, large areas; spreads very rapidly; withstands drought, poor care. Set nursery plants 12–18 inches apart. Some frost damage in high 20°F. temperatures, but quick recovery. *Foliage and flowers:* Gray green, divided leaves grow on plants to 12 inches tall. Yellow daisylike flowers March through summer. Heaviest bloom March–June. See photo on page 62.

ARENARIA balearica. Corsican sandwort. Use between steppingstones or as a small-space lawn substitute in shady, moist areas. *Culture:* Zones B–D, F–H, 6–10; full shade; takes foot traffic; very small areas; fast growing; requires constant moisture. Set nursery plants 3–6 inches apart. *Foliage and flowers:* Oval, thick, glossy leaves to 1/8 inch long in dense mats to 3 inches high. Tiny white flowers in spring, summer.

ARMERIA maritima. Common thrift. Evergreen perennial rather like pink-flowered chives, but stiffer. Needs well-drained soil; will rot where moisture stands at plant base. Use in small areas; good for borders, edging walks. Shear flowers after bloom. *Culture:* Zones A–H, 3–10; full sun; no foot traffic; moderate to rapid growth rate; needs good drainage. Set nursery plants or divisions 6 inches apart, or plant seeds in spring or fall. *Foliage and flowers:* Tufted grassy mounds

spread to 1 foot with stiff 6-inch leaves. Small white to rose pink flowers grow on 6-inch stems in tight round clusters. Blooms almost all year along coastal areas, in spring in other areas. See photo on page 62.

ARUNDINARIA pygmaea (*Sasa*). Bamboo. Low-growing, makes dense ground cover; very invasive and should be confined. Tends to look ragged in winter when old leaves wither. Good for erosion control. *Culture:* Hardy to 0°F.; full sun or partial shade; no foot traffic; good in medium-size areas; fast growing if well watered and fertilized. Set plants 1–2 feet apart. Large, crowded container plants will fill in faster. *Foliage:* Bright green, narrow leaves to 5 inches long; stems, 1/8 inch in diameter, with some purple markings, grow 1–1½ feet tall.

ASARUM caudatum. Wild ginger. Perennial. Native to mild coastal regions of the West. Root has faint ginger odor. Remarkably handsome ground cover in shady areas. *Culture:* Zones B, F, 5–9; full shade; no foot traffic; good for large areas; rapid growth in rich soil, ample moisture; will grow in average soil with some fertilizing, heavy watering. Set nursery plants or divisions 1 foot apart. *Foliage and flowers:* Dark green, heart-shaped leaves 2–7 inches across on stems 10 inches high. With enough water and fertilizer, leaves overlap to hide ground, forming lush carpet. Reddish brown, bell-shaped flowers grow hidden under leaves in spring; somewhat resemble exotic insects. See photo on page 62.

ASPARAGUS densiflorus 'Sprengeri'. Sprenger asparagus. One of several asparagus ferns normally grown in containers, this one grows as a ground cover where temperatures stay above 24° F. *Culture:* Zones F–H, 8–10; full sun to light shade; no foot traffic; good in large areas, on banks; slow to moderate growth rate; survives drought but has better appearance with regular water; grows in ordinary, or even poor, soil. Set nursery plants or divisions 2–4 feet apart. *Foliage and flowers:* Many-branched, feathery stems, 3–6 feet long, billow out from central root mass like a fountain. Branchlets are covered with hard, green, needlelike leaves to 1 inch long. Pinkish white, mildly scented flowers followed by green, then red berries.

Asperula odorata. See Galium

ATRIPLEX semibaccata. Australian saltbush. Fire resistant evergreen ground cover that roots deeply. Excellent for dry, brushy areas. *Culture:* Zones D–H, 8; full sun; no foot traffic; good in large areas or on banks; moderate growth rate; withstands drought, highly alkaline soils. Set nursery plants 3 feet apart. *Foliage and flowers:* Gray green, mounding plant that forms dense mat of foliage 12 inches high, 6 feet across; leaves ½–1½ inches long. Flowers insignificant.

Australian fuchsia. See Correa

Australian saltbush. See Atriplex

Australian violet. See Viola

B

Baby's tears. See Soleirolia

BACCHARIS pilularis. Dwarf coyote brush, dwarf chaparral broom. Excellent fire resistant ground cover native to California coast. Subject to a fungus that may leave bare, burned-looking areas. In its native habitat, a harmless insect causes fruitlike swellings on branch tips. Most dependable of all ground covers in California's high desert. *Culture:* Zones B–D, E (except in warmest parts), F–H, 7–9; sun or light shade; no foot traffic; good in large areas; moderate to rapid growth; withstands a wide range of conditions. Set nursery plants 3–6 feet apart. *Foliage and flowers:* Branches are densely covered with tiny, rounded, toothed, dark green leaves. Billowy and irregular in growth, plants are from 8–24 inches tall, spreading to more than 6 feet across. Flowers insignificant; female plants produce a messy, cottony material. Plants available in most nurseries are cutting-grown from male plants: 'Twin Peaks' ('Twin Peaks #2') has small, dark green leaves, moderate growth rate; 'Pigeon Point' has large, lighter green leaves, grows faster (9 feet wide in 4 years). See photos on pages 51, 63.

Bamboo. See Arundinaria

Bearberry. See Arctostaphylos

Bellflower. See Campanula

BELLIS perennis. English daisy. Perennial; may be grown as an annual. Normally considered a lawn weed, this bright little English daisy makes a pretty cover in meadow areas. Nurseries usually sell improved varieties with double flower forms in pink, rose, red, or white. *Culture:* Zone A–H, 3–10; sun in cool climates, needs shade in hot areas; no foot traffic; best in small areas; moderate growth rate. Needs good soil, regular watering. Set nursery plants 3–6 inches apart. *Foliage and flowers:* Dark green rosettes of 1–2-inch-long leaves that lie flat. Daisies bloom in early spring on 3–6-inch-tall stems. See photo on page 63.

BERGENIA. Perennial; evergreen except in coldest areas. Native to the Himalayas and the mountains of China. Some types will take poor conditions and neglect, but most do better with proper care. None can take foot traffic. All need protection from snails, slugs. Plants form clumps. See photo on page 63.

B. ciliata (*B. ligulata*). *Culture:* Zones A–D, F–H, 3–10; full shade; best in small to medium-size areas; moderate growth rate. Set nursery plants 12 inches apart. Tender foliage may burn in severe frost. *Foliage and flowers:* Light green, lustrous leaves reaching 12 inches long and wide have smooth edges fringed with soft hairs. Young growth is bronzy. White, rose, or purplish flowers in late spring, summer.

B. cordifolia. Heartleaf bergenia. *Culture:* Zones A–D, F–H, 3–10; full shade; best in medium-size areas; can take neglect. Set nursery plants or divisions 12 inches apart. *Foliage and flowers:* Glossy, heart-shaped leaves have wavy-toothed edges; plants grow to 20 inches high. Spring-blooming, rose or lilac flowers hang in clusters from tops of stems, are partially hidden by large leaves.

B. crassifolia. Winter blooming bergenia. *Culture:* Same as *B. cordifolia.* *Foliage and flowers:* Best known bergenia with slightly toothed and wavy, broadly oval, dark green leaves to 8 inches long on short stems. Entire plant may reach 20 inches high. In January and February, dense clusters of rose, lilac, or purple flowers on erect stems stand well above leaves.

Big blue lily turf. See Liriope

Birdsfoot trefoil. See Lotus

Bishop's hat. See Epimedium

Bishop's weed. See Aegopodium

Blue carpet juniper. See Juniperus

Blue fescue. See Festuca

Blue star creeper. See Laurentia

BOUGAINVILLEA. For very warm climates only. Normally trained up a support, these evergreen shrubby vines also will spread out on the ground or trail down a bank; cut out any stems that grow upright. *Culture:* Zones E, F, H, 10; full sun; no foot traffic; rapid growing when established; withstands some midsummer drought. Set nursery plants 6–8 feet apart. CAUTION: Do not remove nursery plants from containers. Bougainvillea roots don't knit soil together in a firm root ball; plant may die if roots are disturbed or exposed during planting. Place can in large planting hole, slit in several places, and carefully pull sides away from soil mass and roots; fill in around roots with soil (buried can will rust away in time). Otherwise you will lose the root soil and kill the plant. *Foliage and flowers:* Dark to medium green leaves along thorny vineline stems. Brilliant in color, "flowers" really papery bracts that bloom through the warm season. Colors range from the common red violet through reds, yellows, oranges, purples, pinks, rose, and white.

Broom. See Cytisus, Genista

Bunchberry. See Cornus

Butcher's broom. See Ruscus

C

California fuchsia. See Zauschneria

CALLUNA vulgaris. Scotch heather. Evergreen shrub; one of three related genera which make up the heaths and heathers. See also *Erica*, page 66. *Culture:* Zones B, F, 5–9; full sun, light shade in hot areas; no foot traffic; best in small to medium-size areas; slow to moderate growth rate; prefers acid, well-drained, moist soil. Growth remains more compact in poor soil. Set nursery plants 12–18 inches apart. *Foliage and flowers:* Choose the lower growing, spreading varieties, ranging from 2–18 inches tall. Foliage is needlelike or scalelike in varying shades from yellowish to dark green. Bell-shaped flowers in spikes range from white through pink, bluish red, to purple, in late summer, fall. May be sheared after flowering to remove dead blooms, stimulate new growth. Of the many varieties, two make good ground covers: 'Mrs. Ronald Gray' forms a creeping mound 3 inches high, has dark foliage, reddish purple flowers in August–September. 'Mullion' in a tight mound to 9 inches, purple flowers August–September.

CAMPANULA. Bellflower. Large family with many plant and flower forms. None take foot traffic. See photos on page 64.

C. carpatica (*C. turbinata*). Tussock bellflower. Perennial. *Culture:* Zones A–D, F, 4–9; full sun or light shade; best in small areas; moderate growth rate; needs acid soil. Set nursery plants or cuttings 6–9 inches apart, or sow seeds. *Foliage and flowers:* Compact tufts of oval, wavy leaves to 1½ inches long with branching and spreading stems. Usually about 8 inches tall, but may reach 12–18 inches. Blue or white flowers in open bells or cups are 1–2 inches across, in late spring. 'Blue Carpet' and 'White Carpet' are dwarf varieties.

C. elatines garganica. Perennial. *Culture:* Zones B–D, F, 7–9; otherwise, same as *C. carpatica.* Set nursery plants about 6 inches apart. *Foliage and flowers:* Low growing plants from 3–6 inches high with small, gray or green, sharply toothed, heart-shaped leaves. Flat, star-shaped, violet blue flowers from June to fall.

C. portenschlagiana. Dalmatian bellflower. Perennial. *Culture:* Zones B–D, F, 5–9; otherwise, same as *C. carpatica.* Set nursery plants 8 inches apart. *Foliage and flowers:* Low mounding mats densely covered with roundish, heart-shaped, deep green leaves with deeply toothed, slightly wavy edges. Flaring violet blue bells to 1 inch long bloom May–August, sometimes again in fall.

C. poscharskyana. Serbian bellflower. Perennial. *Culture:* Zones A–D, F–H, 4–9; shade or sun in cool climates; best in small areas; moderate growth rate; withstands some drought. Set nursery plants 6–12 inches apart. *Foliage and flowers:* Spreading and branching plants with long, heart-shaped, toothed, hairy leaves to 3½ inches long, 3 inches wide. Star-shaped, blue lilac or lavender flowers to 1 inch long on relaxed stems to 1 foot or more long in spring, early summer.

Cape weed. See Arctotheca

CARISSA grandiflora. Natal plum. Large evergreen shrub named for area of South Africa where it is native has several named varieties that are low and spreading. Produces edible fruit. For mild climates only. *Culture:* Zones G, H, 9, 10; either sun or shade; no foot traffic; slow to moderate growth rate; tolerates any soil or exposure. Set nursery plants 3 feet apart and trim upright branches. Slow to establish. *Foliage, flowers, and fruit:* Rich green, glossy, oval leaves about 3 inches long grow on thorny stems. Large, very fragrant 2-inch white flowers shaped like 5-pointed stars bloom over a long season, followed by 1–2-inch, reddish, plum-shaped fruit that can be eaten raw or preserved. 'Green Carpet' grows to about 1½ feet high, spreading to 4 feet across. 'Horizontalis' has dense foliage to 2 feet high; spreads well if upright growth is trimmed; 'Prostrata' is similar. 'Tuttle' ('Nana Compacta Tuttlei') can reach 3 feet high, 5 feet wide; produces many flowers, heavy fruit crop.

Carmel creeper. See Ceanothus

Carolina jessamine. See Gelsemium

Carpet bugle. See Ajuga

Carpobrotus. See Ice plant

Catalina perfume. See Ribes

Catmint. See Nepeta

CEANOTHUS. Wild lilac. Evergreen shrubs with fragrant spring flowers. Most California natives. Drought tolerant; subject to fatal root rots if given regular summer watering. Water infrequently, deeply. Likes well-drained soils. See photos on page 64.

C. gloriosus. Point Reyes ceanothus. Most tolerant ceanothus of ordinary garden watering. *Culture:* Zones B–D, F–H, 8, 9; full sun; no foot traffic; good in large areas; fast growing. Set nursery plants 3–5 feet apart for fast cover. *Foliage and flowers:* Low dense plants to 24 inches tall, 5 feet wide, covered with spiny-toothed, roundish, dark green leaves to 1½ inches long. Rounded, lavender blue flowers in 1-inch clusters. Heavy bloomer. Named varieties are 'Bamico', light green leaves, to 2–3 feet high; 'Emily Brown', 2–3 feet high, to 12 feet wide, violet blue flowers; 'Tuttle', wrinkled hollylike leaves.

C. griseus horizontalis. Carmel creeper. *Culture:* Zones C, D, F–H, 8, 9; otherwise, same as *C. gloriosus.* *Foliage and flowers:* Plants reach 18–30 inches tall, to 15 feet wide. Oval, glossy, bright green leaves to 2 inches long. Light blue flowers in dense clusters. Varieties are 'Compacta', small dense foliage, to 1 foot high, 3 feet across; 'Hurricane Point', does not flower heavily, grows rapidly to 2 feet high, up to 36 feet across; 'Yankee Point', tallest, 2–3 feet high, to 8 feet across, many blue flower clusters.

C. thyrsiflorus repens. Creeping blue blossom. *Culture:* Zones B, F, H, may not be successful east of the Rockies; otherwise same as *C. gloriosus.* *Foliage and flowers:* Glossy, dark green leaves on mat of branches only a few inches high, very wide spreading. Flowers in varying shades of blue, some nearly white. Heavy bloomer.

Cephalophyllum. See Ice plant

CERASTIUM tomentosum. Snow-in-summer. Short-lived perennial. *Culture:* Zones A–H, 3–10; full sun, light shade in warmest areas; no foot traffic; best in small areas, or use in large areas for a few seasons; fast growing; withstands drought; prefers soil with good drainage. Set nursery plants or divisions 12–18 inches apart, or sow seeds. Shear off faded flower clusters. *Foliage and flowers:* Narrow silvery gray leaves in tufted mats to 6 inches tall, 2–3 feet across in one year. Small white flowers from late spring into summer. See photo on page 64.

CERATOSTIGMA plumbaginoides (*Plumbago larpentae*). Dwarf plumbago. Perennial. Performs best if cut back every year. When plants become old or less vigorous, remove them and replace with rooted branches. *Culture:* Zones B–D, F–H, 6–10; full sun to part shade; no foot traffic; good for large areas; moderate to fast growth rate; tolerates any soil type. Set nursery plants or cuttings 18–24 inches apart. Cut back in late winter or early spring when new growth begins. *Foliage and flowers:* Wiry stems with bronzy green to dark green 3-inch leaves that turn red brown with frost. Plants from 6–12 inches tall, spreading rapidly by underground runners in good soil where growing season is long. Clusters of intense blue, ½-inch-wide flowers from July to frost.

CHAMAEMELUM nobile (*Anthemis nobilis*). Chamomile. Evergreen. *Culture:* Zones A–H, 3–10; full sun to very light shade; withstands moderate foot traffic, drought; good in large areas; moderate to rapid growth. Plants mound unevenly. Can be a lawn substitute if mowed or sheared occasionally. Set nursery plants or divisions about 12 inches apart. *Foliage and flowers:* Pale green, finely cut, aromatic leaves in rounded mats, 3–12 inches across, to 12 inches tall if allowed to grow naturally. In summer, surface is covered with yellow, buttonlike flowers; other forms have yellow-centered white daisies.

Chamomile. See Chamaemelum

Checkerberry. See Gaultheria

Cinquefoil. See Potentilla

CISSUS. Grape ivy. Evergreen vines related to Virginia creeper, but without fall color. Require warm climate.

C. antarctica. Kangaroo treebine. *Culture:* Zones F–H, 9–10; sun or shade; no foot traffic; use in small areas; fast growing when established. Set nursery plants 5 feet apart. *Foliage and flowers:* Large, medium green, shiny, slightly toothed leaves from 2–3½ inches long; stems to 10 feet long. Flowers insignificant.

C. hypoglauca. *Culture:* Zones F–H, 10; sun or shade; no traffic; good in large areas, on banks; fast growing when established. Set nursery plants 5 feet apart. *Foliage and flowers:* Highly polished leaves divided into 5 roundish leathery leaflets, each about 3 inches long. Leaves are bronzy; new growth is covered with brownish fuzz. Vines may extend to 30 feet. Flowers insignificant.

C. striata. *Culture:* Zones F–H, 10; sun or shade; no traffic; good bank cover; fast growing when established. Set nursery plants 5 feet apart. *Foliage and flowers:* Like a miniature Virginia creeper. Small leathery leaves divided into 3–5 leaflets, each 1–3 inches long. Stems reddish, up to 10 feet long.

CISTUS salviifolius (*C. villosus* 'Prostratus'). Sageleaf rockrose. Native to Mediterranean region. Sun and heat loving, drought tolerant, will do well where buffeted by ocean wind. Takes regular water if soil is well drained. *Culture:* Zones C, D, E (warmest parts), F–H, 8, 9; full sun; no foot traffic; good for large areas, banks, rough situations; fast growing. Set nursery plants 3 feet apart. *Foliage and flowers:* Low shrub to 2 feet tall, spreads to 6 feet. Light gray green, 1-inch, crinkle-veined leaves. White, 1½-inch flowers have yellow spots at base of petals, bloom profusely in late spring.

Common thrift. See Armeria

Confederate jasmine. See Trachelospermum

Confederate violet. See Viola

CONVALLARIA majalis. Lily-of-the-valley. Forest wildflower in Europe, naturalized in North America. Requires winter chilling; unsatisfactory in mild climates. Makes good carpet under deciduous trees, with other plants needing similar conditions (ca-

mellias, rhododendrons). *Culture:* Zones A–C, 3–7; needs shade; no foot traffic; best in small areas; fast growing; needs soil rich in humus. Set pips (small rootstocks) 4–6 inches apart in late fall, or plant clumps 1–2 feet apart. Top dress yearly with leaf mold, peat moss, or ground bark after foliage has died down. *Foliage and flowers:* Small, white, waxy, very fragrant, bell-shaped flowers hang down from 6–8-inch stems in mid-spring; each plant has two basal leaves to 8 inches long, 3 inches wide.

CONVOLVULUS mauritanicus. Ground morning glory. Evergreen perennial; drought tolerant; especially good on banks or slopes. *Culture:* Zones B–D, F–H, 8, 9; full sun; no foot traffic; fast growing. Set plants 3 feet apart. Plant prefers light gravelly soil with good drainage; will take clay soil if not overwatered. *Foliage and flowers:* Soft, hairy, roundish, gray green leaves to 1½ inches long on trailing branches 1–2 feet high, 3 or more feet wide. Lavender blue, 1–2-inch flowers June–November. See photo on page 46.

COPROSMA kirkii. Stiff, spreading, evergreen shrub that can be clipped low or allowed to grow naturally into a barrier planting (2–3 feet high). *Culture:* Zones D, F–H, 8, 9; sun or partial shade; no foot traffic; good in large areas, on banks; moderate growth rate; tolerates most soil types, wind, sea spray; drought resistant once established. Set nursery plants 2 feet apart; clip vertical growth to keep plant low. *Foliage and flowers:* Small, closely set, yellow green leaves on straight, stiff woody stems. Flowers insignificant. See photo on page 67.

COREOPSIS Perennial ground covers. Established plants can thrive on very little water. See photos on pages 47, 51.

C. auriculata 'Nana'. Dwarf coreopsis. Evergreen in warmer zones, deciduous elsewhere. *Culture:* Zones B–H, 5–10; full sun; no foot traffic; removal of flowers easier in small areas, but plant can be used in large areas; fairly slow growing. Set nursery plants 1 foot apart, or sow seeds. *Foliage and flowers:* Deep green leaves, 2–6 inches long, form 6-inch-high mats. Plant spreads by stolons to about 2 feet wide. Bright orange yellow flowers rise well above foliage, bloom profusely over long season. Remove old flowers with small sickle or lawn mower set at 2–3 inches.

C. verticillata. *Culture:* Zones F–H, 7–10; otherwise same as *C. auriculata* 'Nana'. Very tolerant of drought, neglect. *Foliage and flowers:* Plant is 2½–3 feet tall, half as wide. Many erect or slightly leaning stems carry many whorls of finely divided, very narrow leaves. Bright yellow, 2-inch daisies borne over long summer into fall.

CORNUS canadensis. Bunchberry. Deciduous. A dogwood, but doesn't resemble familiar trees and shrubs except in flowers. Requires cool moist climate. *Culture:* Zones A, B, 3–6; shade; no foot traffic; best in small areas; slow growing; needs acid, humus-rich soil, constant moisture. Set plants or divisions 1 foot apart. Hard to establish, but will establish readily when transplanted with a piece of rotten log with bark attached. *Foliage and flowers:* Creeping rootstocks send up stems topped by whorl of 4–6, oval or roundish, deep rich green, 1–2-inch-long leaves. In fall, leaves yellow, then drop off. Compact cluster of tiny flowers surrounded by 4 oval white bracts (these give appearance of flowers) in May or June. Small, shiny, red berries in August or September. See photo on page 67.

CORONILLA varia. Crown vetch. Perennial. Rather weedy, but a quick cover for bare slopes, remote spots. *Culture:* Zones A–H, 3–10; full sun, will tolerate shade; no foot traffic; best in large areas away from formal gardening; fast growing. Sow seed or set plants 1 foot apart. In spring, mow or scythe, then feed and water for lush growth. Goes dormant and looks ratty during coldest weather. *Foliage and flowers:* Related to clovers, plant spreads by creeping stems, sending out 2-foot stems with compound leaves made up of 11–25 oval leaflets ½–¾ inch long. One-inch clusters of lavender pink flowers soon become bundles of brown, slender, fingerlike seedpods.

CORREA pulchella. Australian fuchsia. Evergreen shrub that needs a warm Mediterranean climate found in parts of California. *Culture:* Zones F–H, 9, 10; full sun, part shade in very hot areas, no reflected heat from walls or paving; no foot traffic; medium to large areas, especially good on banks or slopes; moderate growth rate; must have perfect drainage, will grow in poor or rocky soil. Won't tolerate too much watering or fertilizing. Set nursery plants 2–4 feet apart. *Foliage and*

Climate Zone Maps, pages 42–43

ACHILLEA tomentosa
Sun-loving, easy-to-maintain achillea has grayish
green fernlike foliage; flat clusters of yellow flowers
appear in summer. (See page 56.)

AJUGA reptans
Lustrous leaves, dark green to purplish, form
thick, low cover. Foliage mat topped with blue to
purplish flowers on spikes in spring, early summer.
(See page 56.)

AGAPANTHUS
Good for borders, edgings, streetside areas,
agapanthus' clumps of strap-shaped leaves,
blue flower globes on tall stalks in summer,
give exotic look to garden. (See page 56.)

ARMERIA maritima
Low grassy mounds fill in borders, edgings, small areas in sun. Pink flower clusters appear in spring. (See page 57.)

ARCTOTHECA calendula
Perfect for large, hard-to-reach areas in mild climates. Grows rapidly in full sun, tolerates drought, minimal care. Yellow daisylike flowers bloom in spring, summer. (See page 57.)

ARCTOSTAPHYLOS
uva-ursi
Whether draping over walls (right), trailing down hillsides, or growing along ground (above), glossy, leathery leaves of arctostaphylos create a handsome cover. (See pages 56–57.)

ASARUM caudatum
Handsome foliage plant for shady, moist areas. (See page 57.)

BERGENIA crassifolia
Best-known bergenia has large, handsome, dark green foliage, dense clusters of pink flowers in winter. (See page 58.)

BACCHARIS pilularis
Adaptable, dependable cover for sunny hillsides. Plants grow in many climates, soil types, in swampy conditions or drought in coastal areas; form billowy mat of small, dense, bright green leaves. (See page 58.)

BELLIS perennis
Grown with grass or alone, perky daisies add light touch to landscape. Nurseries also carry improved varieties with double flowers. (See page 58.)

CAMPANULA poscharskyana
Climbing, spreading plant grows in
light shade (left) or sun. Violet blue,
star-shaped flowers (above) bloom in
spring through early summer.
(See page 59.)

**CEANOTHUS
griseus horizontalis**
Fast-growing, spreading cover for
hillsides, large areas; drought
tolerant in well-drained soil. Dark
green, shiny foliage (right) offers interesting contrast to pink ice plant.
Blue ceanothus flowers (below) form
in clusters in spring. (See page 59.)

CERASTIUM tomentosum
Useful in small areas, or between shrubs or other
slow-growing ground covers, cerastium's
silvery gray foliage stands out nicely
against brick, green plants. White blooms
are profuse from late spring into summer.
(See page 59.)

flowers: Branches grow to 2–2½ feet tall, spread up to 8 feet wide. Small roundish 1-inch leaves are green above, densely felted gray green beneath. Small, bell-shaped, pale pink flowers hang down along branches November–April.

Corsican sandwort. See Arenaria

COTONEASTER. (Pronounced kuh-TOE-nee-ass-ter.) Deciduous or evergreen plants; thrive on neglect. Don't plant along walks or drives where branch ends will need pruning; stubbed branches unattractive. None of the cotoneasters take foot traffic. See photos on pages 50, 67.

C. adpressus. Creeping cotoneaster. Deciduous. *Culture:* Zones A–H, 5–9; full sun to part shade; good in large or medium-size areas, on banks; slow growing. Set nursery plants 3 feet apart; plant annuals or wildflowers in between for several seasons until ground cover fills in. *Foliage and flowers:* Smooth, dark green, ½-inch leaves turn red in fall, then drop off. Plants eventually reach 1 foot high, 8 feet across, but it may take 5 or 6 years. Pink tinted flowers followed by showy, ¼-inch red fruit. *C. a. praecox* has leaves, fruit twice as large.

C. conspicuus 'Decorus'. Necklace cotoneaster. Evergreen. *Culture:* Zones B–H, 7–9; full sun to part shade; good in small to medium-size areas; moderate growth rate; set nursery plants 3 feet apart. *Foliage and flowers:* Narrow, oval leaves ¼-inch long, dark green, pale undersides. White flowers followed by ⅜-inch red fruit.

C. dammeri. Bearberry cotoneaster. Evergreen. *Culture:* Zones A–H, 5–9; full sun to partial shade; no foot traffic; good for medium to large areas; moderate to rapid growth. Set nursery plants 5 feet apart. *Foliage and flowers:* Long prostrate branches root where they touch the soil. Plants reach 6 inches tall, spread to 10 feet across. Oval, 1-inch-long, glossy, bright green leaves are whitish beneath. Profusion of white flowers followed by showy, ½-inch red fruit. The variety 'Lowfast' is vigorous and spreads as much as 2 feet a year, reaching 10–15 feet across, but stays 1 foot high. Smaller leaves (to ¾ inch long) are dark green above, grayish green beneath; less dense. 'Coral Beauty' has coral fruit; 'Red Beauty' has red fruit. 'Skogsholmen' resembles a stiffer, slightly taller, hardier 'Lowfast'.

C. horizontalis. Rock cotoneaster. Deciduous. *Culture:* Zones A–H, 5–9; full sun to part shade; no foot traffic; good in medium to large areas; mod-erate growth rate. Give plant room to spread; set nursery plants 5–10 feet apart. *Foliage and flowers:* Deciduous for a short time in winter; leaves turn orange and red before they fall. Plant reaches 2–3 feet high, spreading to 15 feet across. Growth habit is stiff and angular, the branches arranged in flat planes, herringbone fashion. White flowers followed by dense clusters of small red fruit. Variety 'Robustus' is taller, with larger foliage and fruit. 'Variegatus' has white-edged leaves. *C. h. perpusillus* is flatter, more compact, with ¼-inch leaves.

C. microphyllus. Rockspray cotoneaster. Evergreen. *Culture:* Zones B–H, 6–9; full sun to partial shade; no foot traffic; medium to large areas, good on banks if not overwatered or overfertilized; moderate growth rate. Set nursery plants 3 feet apart. *Foliage and flowers:* Both trailing and upright branches. Main stems trail to 6 feet or more, also send up vertical branches that reach 2–3 feet high; cut back upright branches to keep plant low. Tiny dark green leaves have gray hair beneath. White flowers followed by small, long-lasting, rosy red fruit. Variety 'Cooperi' is especially small in leaf; 'Emerald Spray' is resistant to fire-blight. *C. m. cochleatus* is more compact, more prostrate, with broader and paler leaves.

C. salicifolius 'Herbstfeuer'. Evergreen to semi-evergreen. *Culture:* Zones B–H, 7–9; full sun to part shade; no foot traffic; good in medium to large areas; moderate growth rate. Set nursery plants 4–6 feet apart. *Foliage and flowers:* Prostrate plants 6 inches high, spreading to 8 feet across. Narrow, willowlike, wrinkled leaves are dark green above, grayish beneath, to 3½ inches long. Clustered white flowers followed by small orange red fruit. *C. s.* 'Repens' has narrower leaves, bright red fruit.

COTULA squalida. New Zealand brass buttons. Evergreen perennial. *Culture:* Zones B–D, G, H, 8–10; full sun to partial shade; no foot traffic; good in small to large areas; rapid growth rate. Set nursery plants or divisions about 6 inches apart. *Foliage and flowers:* Plants stay a few inches high, spreading to 1 foot or more across. Soft, hairy, fernlike, bronzy green leaves. Summer flowers are tight yellow heads like ¼-inch brass buttons.

Cranesbill. See Erodium

CRASSULA multicava. Succulent, related to the jade plant. Needs a warm winter. *Culture:* Zones F, H, 9, 10; grows well in full sun or shade; no foot traffic; best in small or medium-size areas; rampant grower. Set cuttings, divisions, or nursery plants 1 foot apart in any type soil. *Foliage and flowers:* Dark green fleshy leaves on spreading stems. Light pink, mosquitolike flowers in late winter, spring. May not flower unless grown in full sun.

Creeping blue blossom. See Ceanothus

Creeping buttercup. See Ranunculus

Creeping cotoneaster. See Cotoneaster

Creeping fig. See Ficus

Creeping Jennie. See Lysimachia

Creeping lily turf. See Liriope

Creeping mahonia. See Mahonia

Creeping snowberry. See Symphoricarpos

Creeping thyme. See Thymus

Creeping wire vine. See Muehlenbeckia

Crown vetch. See Coronilla

CYMBALARIA. Creeping perennial plants related to snapdragons. Can be invasive under ideal conditions. See photo on page 45.

C. aequitriloba. *Culture:* Zones D, F–H, 8–10; needs full shade; no foot traffic; best in small areas; fast growing; needs good soil, ample water. Plant cuttings 6 inches apart, or sow seeds in spring. Stems root where they touch soil. *Foliage and flowers:* Inch-deep mat that looks like small-scale dichondra. Leaves slightly 3–5-lobed. Tiny purple snapdragonlike flowers.

C. muralis (*Linaria cymbalaria*). Kenilworth ivy. Perennial usually grown as an annual; succumbs to hard freezes or long droughts. *Culture:* Zones B–D, F, H, 4–10; otherwise, same as *C. aequitriloba*. *Foliage and flowers:* Small, smooth, kidney-shaped leaves with 3–7 toothlike lobes. Tiny lilac blue flowers marked with white and yellow, shaped like snapdragons, spring to fall.

CYTISUS kewensis. Kew broom. Also see *Genista*, page 72. *Culture:* Zones B, F, 6–8; full sun; no foot traffic; best in small to medium-size areas; moderate growth rate; needs good drainage; tolerates wind, poor soil, drought. Set nursery plants 2 feet apart. *Foliage and flowers:* Prostrate plant stays under 1 foot high, spreads to 4 feet or more. Sweetpealike, creamy white, ½-inch flowers April–May.

D

Dalmatian bellflower. See Campanula

Daylily. See Hemerocallis

Delosperma. See Ice plant

DIANTHUS. Pinks. Small-scale ground cover with bright, often fragrant flowers, grassy mounding foliage.

D. deltoides. Maiden pink. Perennial. *Culture:* Zones A–D, F–H, 3–10; full sun; no foot traffic; best confined to small areas; slow growth rate; needs light, rich, non-acid, well drained soil. Set plants or rooted cuttings 4–6 inches apart. *Foliage and flowers:* Rough light green foliage forms loose, low, grassy mats with ¾-inch flowers on stems 8–12 inches tall; blooms in summer, sometimes repeating bloom in fall. Shear flowers when they fade. Flowers range from shades of rose to purple and white, spotted with lighter colors.

D. 'Tiny Rubies'. Perennial. *Culture:* Same as *D. deltoides. Foliage and flowers:* Gray tufts grow 3 inches tall, spread to 4 inches. Foliage is attractive all year. Small double ruby red flowers in summer.

Dittany of Crete. See Origanum

Drosanthemum. See Ice plant

DUCHESNEA indica. Indian mock strawberry. Perennial. Resembles strawberry, with similar foliage and trailing stems that root along the ground, but unlike the strawberry, its flowers and fruit stand above the leaves. *Culture:* Zones A–H, 3–10; either sun or shade (good under trees); can take some foot traffic; good in medium to large areas; fast growing. Set nursery plants or rooted stolons 12–18 inches apart. Trim in spring to keep neat. In shade, plant stems tend to be longer, and bloom is reduced. *Foliage and flowers:* Bright green, long-stalked leaves with 3 leaflets are indistinguishable from strawberry leaves. Bright yellow, ½-inch flowers followed by red, flavorless raspberry-size fruit.

Dune manzanita. See Arctostaphylos

Dwarf coreopsis. See Coreopsis

Dwarf lily-of-the-Nile. See Agapanthus

E

English daisy. See Bellis

English ivy. See Hedera

EPIMEDIUM. Perennial plants for wooded areas; good with rhododendrons, azaleas, or camellias. Makes a lacy, rather than solid, ground cover.

E. grandiflorum. Bishop's hat, longspur epimedium. *Culture:* Zones A–D, F, 3–8; filtered shade; no foot traffic; best in small areas; moderate growth rate; prefers acid, humus-rich soil. Set nursery plants or divisions 1 foot apart, in spring or fall. Clip off old leaves in early spring. *Foliage and flowers:* Thin, wiry stems bear heart-shaped leaflets to 3 inches long that unfold bronzy pink, turn green, then bronze with cold weather. Loose spikes of 1–2 inch flowers bloom in spring, with sepals red and violet, petals white and long spurred. Varieties available with white, pinkish, or violet flowers.

E. pinnatum. *Culture:* Same as *E. grandiflorum. Foliage and flowers:* Plants a few inches taller than *E. grandiflorum;* flowers smaller, with yellow sepals and red petals.

E. rubrum. *Culture:* Same as *E. grandiflorum. Foliage and flowers:* Like *E. grandiflorum,* foliage bears showy clusters of flowers with bright crimson sepals; pale yellow or white, slipperlike petals, up-curved spurs. 'Pink Queen', rosy pink flowers, and 'Snow Queen', white, are varieties sometimes found in specialty nurseries.

ERICA. Heath. Like related heathers (see *Calluna,* pages 58–59), these evergreen shrubs have small needlelike leaves and an abundance of small bell-shaped flowers. See photos on pages 49, 50, 68.

E. carnea. *Culture:* Zones B–D, F–H, 6–8; sun or part shade in hot climates; no foot traffic; good for small to large areas; moderate growth rate; prefers acid soil, good drainage, constant moisture; tolerates slightly alkaline soil. Sandy soil lightened with peat moss, compost ideal; heavy clay usually fatal. Needs pruning annually; shear when blooms fade. *Foliage and flowers:* Plants 6–16 inches tall with prostrate branches producing upright branchlets that may be pruned. Medium green leaves; rosy red flowers, December–June. Varieties include: 'Ruby Glow', to 8 inches tall, ruby red bloom; 'Springwood', to 8 inches, dark green leaves, white or creamy bloom; 'Springwood Pink', to 10 inches, pink bloom; 'Vivellii', to 12 inches, bronzy foliage in winter, carmine red bloom; 'Winter Beauty', to 15 inches, dark green foliage, deep pink bloom.

E. ciliaris. Dorset heath. *Culture:* Zones B, F, 8; otherwise, same as *E. carnea.* Set nursery plants 1 foot apart. *Foliage and flowers:* Trailing plant from 6–12 inches tall, pale green leaves, rosy-red flowers July–September. Varieties include: 'Mrs. C. H. Gill', dark green foliage, showy red flowers; 'Stoborough', taller, to 18 inches, white flowers July–October.

E. cinerea. Twisted heath. *Culture:* Zones B, F, 6–8; otherwise, same as *E. carnea. Foliage and flowers:* Spreading mounds to 12 inches tall with dark green, dainty leaves. Purple flowers in summer. Varieties include: 'Atrosanguinea', spreading growth, to 9 inches tall, slow growing, scarlet flowers; 'C.D. Eason', to 10 inches, red flowers May–August; 'G. Ford', to 8 inches, deep red flowers; 'P.S. Patrick', taller, to 15 inches, long spikes of large purple flowers.

E. 'Dawn'. *Culture:* Same as *E. carnea. Foliage and flowers:* Cross between *E. ciliaris* and *E. tetralix.* Easy to grow; forms a spreading mound to 12 inches tall. New growth golden, turning green; deep pink flowers in summer, early fall.

E. tetralix. Cross-leafed heath. Two varieties below serve as ground covers.

E. t. 'Darleyensis'. *Culture:* Zones B, F, 4–8; otherwise, same as *E. carnea. Foliage and flowers:* Spreading open growth to 8 inches tall; gray green leaves; salmon pink flowers in summer.

E. t. 'Praegerae'. *Culture:* Same as *E. carnea. Foliage and flowers:* Spreading growth to 6 inches tall; somewhat greener than *E. t. 'Darleyensis';* bright pink flowers summer, early fall.

ERIGERON karvinskianus (often called *Vittadinia*). Mexican native with daisylike flowers on trailing branches. Tolerates root competition from other plants; naturalizes easily; can be invasive unless controlled. Best for informal effects. *Culture:* Zones D–H, 9; full sun; no foot traffic; good in small or medium-size areas; fast growth rate; likes sandy soil, moderate watering. Drought tolerant. Set nursery plants 1 foot apart. Shear

(Continued on page 71)

COTONEASTER

These covers thrive on neglect. Cotoneaster dammeri 'Lowfast' (below) is vigorous, spreads rapidly, has small dark green leaves, white flowers followed by red berries. Cotoneaster salicifolius 'Herbstfeuer' (left) has narrow, wrinkled leaves, dark green above, grayish underneath. (See page 65.)

COPROSMA kirkii
Hardy shrub tolerates most soils, wind, drought.
Narrow leaves on stiff branches. (See page 60.)

CORNUS canadensis
Good cover for cool, moist climates. Red berries
follow white dogwoodlike flowers. (See page 60.)

ERICA

Evergreen shrubs come in a wide selection of foliage colors, flower colors. If chosen and planted carefully, can achieve tapestry effect shown here. (See page 66.)

ERIGERON karvinskianus

Fast-growing, drought-tolerant, trailing cover with daisylike flowers for sunny spots. White or pink blossoms with yellow centers, early summer into fall. (See pages 66, 71.)

EUONYMUS fortunei

One of the most popular evergreen foliage ground covers. Plants will tolerate moist, acid soils. Euonymus fortunei 'Gracilis' (above left) is grown for variegated foliage. Euonymus fortunei 'Kewensis' (above right) has tiny, dense leaves that create a fine-textured cover. (See page 71.)

GAZANIA

Trailing or clumping ground covers grown for brilliant flower color. Choices include (left, top to bottom) Row 1: 'Fiesta Red', 'Sunburst', clumping yellow; Row 2: trailing orange, trailing white; Row 3: 'Sunrise Yellow', clumping white, 'Aztec Queen'; Row 4: trailing yellow, 'Moonglow'; Row 5: 'Copper King', 'Gold Rush', clumping orange. Mass planting (below) is spectacular in full bloom. (See page 72.)

FRAGARIA chiloensis

Low-growing, rapidly spreading cover has glossy, dark green leaves with three leaflets, resembling strawberry plants. Tolerates light foot traffic. (See page 71.)

GALIUM odoratum

Whorls of light green leaves form shade-loving cover that prefers rich, acid soil, lots of water. Clusters of tiny white flowers in late spring, early summer. Good under trees. (See page 71.)

HEDERA

For the gardener who wants maximum coverage
with minimal effort. Fast-growing; will tolerate
almost any growing situation from full sun to deep
shade; makes few cultural demands. Hedera
canariensis (above) provides shiny green foliage
over large areas, hillsides. Variegated leaf form is
available too. Hedera helix (left) is finer textured
and less aggressive than Hedera canariensis, and
needs less water. Has many varieties with varying
leaf shapes. (See page 73.)

HEDERA helix
This landscape situation takes advantage of
hedera's two growth habits: spreading and climbing. Lacy effect of ivy tendrils helps soften
wall, and ground-hugging vines form dense cover
for soil. Design: R. David Adams. (See page 73.)

plants after bloom fades. *Foliage and flowers:* Long trailing stems with 1-inch leaves, fairly sparse, toothed at tip. Can reach 10–20 inches tall. Dainty flowers ¾ inch across with white or pinkish rays, yellow centers. See photo on page 68.

ERODIUM chamaedryoides. Cranesbill. From Mediterranean islands, dainty perennial related to geranium. *Culture:* Zones C, D, F–H, 7–10; full sun or light shade; light foot traffic; best in small areas; slow growth rate; needs ample moisture. Set nursery plants 6 inches apart. *Foliage and flowers:* Roundish, ⅓-inch-long, scalloped, dark green leaves form dense tuft 12 inches across, 3–6 inches tall. Profuse, cup-shaped, ½-inch-wide, white or pink flowers with pink veins, April–October.

EUONYMUS fortunei (*E. radicans acuta*). Winter creeper. Evergreen vine. Many varieties of *E. fortunei* are good ground covers. No foot traffic. See photos on page 68.

E. f. 'Azusa'. *Culture:* Zones A–F, 5–10; either sun or shade; no foot traffic; good in large areas; slow to moderate growth rate; tolerates moist, acid soil. Set nursery plants 24 inches apart; mulch new plantings heavily to control weeds. Good prostrate growth habit. *Foliage and flowers:* Small, dark green leaves with light colored veins; undersides turn maroon in winter. Flowers unimportant.

E. f. 'Colorata'. Purple-leaf winter creeper. *Culture:* Same as *E. f.* 'Azusa'. *Foliage:* Leaves turn dark purple in fall, winter. Makes a more even carpet then *E. f. radicans*.

E. f. 'Gracilis' (often sold as *E. radicans argentea variegata, E. f. variegata, E. f.* 'Silver Edge'). Less vigorous, restrained growth habit. Best in small areas. *Culture:* Same as *E. f.* 'Azusa'. *Foliage:* Leaves variegated with white or cream; lighter portions turn pinkish in fall, winter.

E. f. 'Kewensis' (*E. f.* 'Minima'). *Culture:* Same as *E. f.* 'Azusa'. *Foliage:* Tiny, dense, ¼-inch leaves create a fine-textured ground cover.

E. f. radicans. Common winter creeper. Tough, hardy, trailing or vining shrub. *Culture:* Same as *E. f.* 'Azusa'. *Foliage:* Dark green, thick-textured, 1-inch-long leaves. Trim to maintain even height. Good on steep banks.

Evergreen candytuft. See Iberis

Evergreen currant. See Ribes

F

FATSHEDERA lizei. Evergreen. Cross between *Fatsia japonica* and *Hedera helix.* Tends to be shrubby as well as creeping; needs protection from sun and wind except along coast. *Culture:* Zones B–H, 8–10; leaves injured at 15° F.; prefers partial shade, will tolerate heavy shade; good in large areas; needs lots of water. Set nursery plants 3 feet apart; cut down upright growth whenever you see it. *Foliage:* Large polished leaves with 3–5 large lobes to 8 inches across. Variety 'Variegata' leaves have white margins. Heavy, knobby stems show through foliage.

FESTUCA ovina 'Glauca'. Blue fescue. Decorative, blue gray grass related to lawn fescues; will not make turf; needs regular weeding, grooming. Old clumps can be divided. *Culture:* Zones A–H, 4–9; full sun or light shade; no foot traffic; best in small to medium-size areas; fast growing; needs little water except in desert areas; won't tolerate wet soil. Set nursery plants or divisions 6–15 inches apart depending on density desired. Shear to 2 inches high after flowering. *Foliage and flowers:* Blue gray tufts of grass 4–10 inches tall. Flowers, seed heads insignificant.

FICUS pumila. Creeping fig. Not at all figlike, this vigorous, tough vine clings to anything. Roots invasive. Dislikes heat on southern or western exposures. *Culture:* Zones D–H, 9, 10; full sun, will yellow in high heat; no foot traffic; good in medium to large areas; slow to start, then vigorous. Set nursery plants 1–2 feet apart; cut back severely in a few weeks to force young growth. Prune out coarse upright branches. Don't let plant climb trees or shrubs—it will overwhelm them in time. *Foliage and fruit:* Young leaves small and glossy; on mature plants, leathery oblong leaves can reach 4 inches long. Large, inedible oblong fruit forms on mature plants. Variety 'Minima' is a small-leafed form.

Firethorn. See Pyracantha

Forget-me-not. See Myosotis

FRAGARIA chiloensis. Wild strawberry, sand strawberry. Evergreen. Native to Pacific Coast of North and South America. Normally does not set fruit. *Culture:* Zones B–H, 6–10; full sun along coast, or light shade; very

light foot traffic; good in small or large areas; fast growing; may need extra iron (sulfate or chelate) if leaves yellow in late summer; water regularly. Set nursery plants or stolons (plantlets from runners) 12–18 inches apart. Plant stolons in late spring, nursery plants any time. Plant needs annual mowing or cutting back in early spring to force new growth, prevent buildup of old stems. *Foliage and flowers:* Glossy, dark green leaves with three leaflets form low, compact mats 6–12 inches tall. Foliage turns reddish in cold weather. Plants send out runners with strings of plantlets that root where they touch soil. Will cascade over banks or walls. White, 1-inch flowers in spring may be followed by seedy red fruit under leaves in fall. See photo on page 69.

G

GALAX urceolata (*G. aphylla*). Good perennial for shady situations. Leaves frequently used in indoor arrangements. *Culture:* Zones A, B, 3–8; full shade; no foot traffic; best in small to medium-size areas; slow growing; must have acid soil with lots of organic matter. Set nursery plants 12 inches apart. *Foliage and flowers:* Clumps of shiny heart-shaped leaves 5 inches across on stalks to 9 inches high; leaves turn bronze in fall. Flower spikes 2½ feet tall with small white flowers in July.

GALIUM odoratum (*Asperula odorata*). Sweet woodruff. *Culture:* Zones A, B, F, 5–10; full shade; no foot traffic; best in small areas or as sparse cover in large areas under trees; rapid growth in rich soil; prefers acid soil, abundant moisture. Set nursery plants or root divisions 1 foot apart. Self-sows freely. *Foliage and flowers:* Square, 6–12-inch stems encircled by whorls of light green, bristle-tipped leaves. Leaves aromatic when dried. Clusters of tiny white flowers at stem ends in late spring, early summer. See photo on page 69.

Garden verbena. See Verbena

GARDENIA jasminoides 'Radicans'. Evergreen shrub. Best in warm-summer climates with fairly mild winters. Flowers have strong fragrance. *Culture:* Zones C–F, H, 8, 9; partial or filtered shade, full sun in western coastal areas; give north or east exposure in desert; no foot traffic; good in small to medium-size areas; moderate growth rate; plant on slight mound to avoid crown rot. Set nursery plants 1–2 feet apart. *Foliage and flowers:* Woody plants 6–12 inches high, spreading to 3 feet. Small, glossy, dark green leaves often streaked with white. Very fragrant, double, 1-inch wide white flowers in summer.

GAULTHERIA. Evergreen, acid-loving plants, happy in same conditions as rhododendrons and azaleas. None take foot traffic.

G. ovatifolia. Native to mountains from Northern California to British Columbia. *Culture:* Zones B, C, F, 6–8; needs light shade; best in small woodland areas; moderate growth rate. Set nursery plants 12 inches apart; keep mulched and weeded until established. *Foliage, flowers, and fruit:* Trailing, spreading plant with upright branches to 8 inches tall. Oval, leathery, dark green leaves to 1½-inches long. Tiny white to pinkish flowers in summer, followed by scarlet, edible, wintergreen-flavored berries that attract birds.

G. procumbens. Wintergreen, checkerberry, teaberry. Native to eastern United States. *Culture:* Zones A–C, 4–8; otherwise, same as G. ovatifolia. *Foliage, flowers, and fruit:* Spreads by creeping stems. Upright branches to 6 inches high bear oval, glossy, 2-inch leaves, clustered toward tips. Small, white, summer flowers followed by scarlet berries lasting into winter. Leaves and berries have wintergreen flavor; both are tasty.

GAZANIA. Perennial. Two types, clumping and trailing; many color forms in each type. All provide brilliant color in late spring, early summer; will bloom sporadically throughout the year where winters are mildest. *Culture:* Zones D–H, generally not successful east of the Rockies; full sun; no foot traffic; good in small to large areas depending on type; fast growing; takes poor soil; needs only moderate amount of water except in desert areas. Use clumping types in small plantings, as filler among young shrubs, in parking strips; trailing types good as larger scale cover for level ground or banks. *Foliage and flowers:* Clumping gazania forms mound of leaves, dark green above, gray and woolly underneath. Daisylike, 3–4-inch-wide flowers on 6–10-inch stems. Flower colors range from yellow to orange, white, or pink with purplish

underneath; several colors may be mixed on single flower. Varieties include 'Copper King', basically orange with markings in several colors; 'Burgundy'; 'Fiesta Red'; 'Aztec Queen', multicolored; 'Moonglow', double, yellow; 'Gold Rush'. Trailing gazania (G. uniflora, may be sold as G. leucolaena) has silvery gray foliage, grows to same height as clumping kinds but spreads rapidly on long creeping stems. Abundant flowers in yellow, orange, white, or bronze, to 2½ inches across. Several varieties excel in length of bloom season, flower size, dieback resistance. Among these are 'Sunburst', orange with black center; 'Sunglow', yellow; and 'Sunrise Yellow', green-leafed, yellow flowers with black centers. See photos on page 69.

GELSEMIUM sempervirens. Carolina jessamine. Shrubby evergreen vine with fragrant flowers. All parts of plant poisonous. *Culture:* Zones D–H, 8–10; full sun; no foot traffic; use in medium-size areas; moderate growth rate; trim in spring if needed to keep low. Best with regular water, but tolerates some drought. Set nursery plants 2–3 feet apart. Will twine up into shrubs and trees if not controlled. *Foliage and flowers:* Shiny, light green, 1–4-inch-long pairs of leaves on stems to 20 feet. Yellow, tubular, fragrant 1½-inch-long flowers in late winter or early spring.

GENISTA. Broom. Also see Cytisus, page 65. Usually deciduous, but green branches give plant evergreen look. Flowers shaped like sweet peas. Dwarf and prostrate brooms rare in nurseries; check with rock garden plant specialists.

G. hispanica. Spanish broom. Good low barrier plant. *Culture:* Zones B–G, 8; full sun; no foot traffic; best in small to medium-size areas; moderate growth rate; needs good drainage; give infrequent deep watering in dry summers. Cool summer weather best for most brooms. Set nursery plants 2 feet apart. *Foliage and flowers:* Mass of very spiny stems with ½-inch leaves. Grows 1–2 feet tall, spreading wide. Golden yellow flowers at branch tips in May, June.

G. lydia. (Often sold as Cytisus lydia.) *Culture:* Zone B; otherwise, same as G. hispanica. *Foliage and flowers:* Not very hardy. To 2 feet tall, spreading wide. Profuse, bright yellow flowers at branch tips in June. Sets very few seed pods.

G. pilosa. *Culture:* Same as G. hispanica. *Foliage and flowers:* Fairly

fast growing to 1–1½ feet tall with 7-foot spread. Branches root where they touch soil. Intricately branching gray green twigs with roundish leaves to ½ inch long. Yellow flowers in May, June.

G. sagittalis. *Culture:* Same as G. hispanica. *Flowers and foliage:* Fast growing to 12 inches tall, spreading wide. Upright, winged, bright green branchlets appear jointed. Profuse bloom creates sheet of golden yellow in late spring, early summer.

Geranium, common or florists'. See Pelargonium

GERANIUM incanum. Unlike florists' geraniums and pelargoniums, true geraniums are usually delicate, small-flowered plants. Recently introduced, this geranium ground cover may be hard to find. *Culture:* Zones D, F–H, 9, 10; full sun; no foot traffic; best in small areas; fast growing. Set nursery plants 4–6 inches apart in rock gardens, over bulb beds, or in small areas where you want a delicate, natural effect. *Foliage and flowers:* Finely lobed, lacelike leaves on delicate stems to 6–8 inches tall. Showy, ½-inch, red violet flowers through summer.

Germander. See Teucrium

GLECHOMA hederacea. Ground ivy, Gill-over-the-ground. May be considered a weed, especially in moist shady areas. *Culture:* Zones A–H, 4–10; full shade; some foot traffic; best in small to medium-size areas; fast growing. Set nursery plants 12 inches apart, or encourage volunteer plants in shady areas. *Foliage and flowers:* Long creeping stems root at joints in moist places; plant reaches 3–6 inches tall. Round, bright green leaves with coarsely scalloped edges. Light blue flowers in spring, summer.

Goldmoss sedum. See Sedum

Gout-weed. See Aegopodium

Greek yarrow. See Achillea

Green carpet. See Herniaria

GREVILLEA lanigera. Woolly grevillea. Evergreen. For tall cover on banks or as barrier planting. Best in mild-winter climates with hot dry summers; not good in areas with humid summers or where plants receive too much summer water. *Culture:* Zones F–H, not generally successful east of the Rockies; full sun; no foot traffic; good for large areas; moderate growth rate; prefers well-drained soil, moderate watering for young plants; tolerates drought, poor soil when established. Set nursery plants 3–4 feet apart. *Foliage and flowers:* Spreading mounding plants, 3–6 feet tall, 6–10 feet wide. Narrow, closely set, gray green ½-inch leaves. Profuse clusters of narrow-petaled crimson and cream flowers in summer; attract birds.

Ground ivy. See Glechoma

Hall's Japanese honeysuckle. See Lonicera

Heartleaf bergenia. See Bergenia

HEBE. Evergreen. Prefers mild, cool-summer climates. Hot summers shorten plant's lifespan, but it will grow in partial shade.

H. chathamica. *Culture:* Zones F–H, not generally successful east of the Rockies; full sun where summers are cool, partial shade in hot climates; no foot traffic; fast growing; best in small to medium-size areas; must have excellent drainage, regular watering. Will tolerate wind and salt air in coastal areas. Set nursery plants 18 inches apart. *Foliage and flowers:* Little shrubs to 1½ feet tall, spreading to 3 feet across. Deep green, ½-inch leaves. Feathery lavender flowers on 1-inch spikes in summer.

H. pinguifolia 'Pagei'. *Culture:* Zones B, F, H; otherwise, same as *H. chathamica.* Set nursery plants 2–3 feet apart. *Foliage and flowers:* Grows to 9 inches tall, 5 feet wide. Blue gray, ½-inch leaves edged with rose. Fat white flower spikes to 1 inch long in summer.

HEDERA. Ivy. Evergreen woody vines. When used as a ground cover, hedera should be cut away from trees and shrubs; prune it to the ground every few seasons in early spring. Ivy climbs anything by aerial rootlets, and even will try to get into a house through cracks; stems become woody, thick as they age. Ground cover ivy provides breeding ground for slugs and snails (use bait) and in some areas, rats. See photos on pages 50, 70.

H. canariensis. Algerian ivy. *Culture:* Zones D–H, 8–10; either sun or shade; no foot traffic, but you can wade through it without damage; good in medium to large areas; slow to start, then fast growing. Cut back to the ground when too many thick stems form, using a rugged rotary mower, hedge shears, or machete. Set nursery plants 18 inches apart and keep soil moist. Mulch heavily while plants establish. Trim edges with heavy shears 2 or 3 times a season. For best growth, appearance, feed with high-nitrogen fertilizer twice a year in early spring and midsummer. In hot-summer areas, plant needs regular watering. *Foliage:* Shiny green leaves (green and white in variety 'Variegata') up to 8 inches across with 3–5 shallow lobes; leaves widely spaced along stems.

H. helix. English ivy. Finer textured, less aggressive than Algerian ivy, and needs less moisture. Can be used in smaller areas. *Culture:* Zones A–H, 6–10; otherwise, same as *H. canariensis. Foliage:* Leaves dark green, not shiny, 2–4 inches long and wide. Variety 'Baltica' very hardy with much smaller, whitish-veined leaves that turn purplish in winter; 'Hahn's Self Branching' is more densely branched, has lighter green leaves; best in part shade.

HELIANTHEMUM nummularium. Sunrose. Evergreen spreading shrublet with abundant colorful bloom. *Culture:* Zones A–H, 5–10; full sun; no foot traffic; small to medium-size areas; slow to start, moderate growth rate; needs perfect drainage; tolerates heat, infrequent watering (in hot-summer areas may need more water). Set nursery plants 1–2 feet apart; mulch heavily to control weeds. Where winters are cold, mulch with evergreen boughs to keep plants from dehydrating. Shear after spring bloom to encourage fall flowers. *Foliage and flowers:* Woody plants with gray green leaves, or green leaves with fuzzy gray backs, to 8 inches tall, 3 feet wide. One-inch-wide, single or double flowers (depending on variety), in flame, red, apricot, orange, yellow, pink, rose, peach, salmon, or white. They last only a day, but new ones open continually over a 2–3 month period, April–June in mild-winter regions, May–July in cold winters. See photo on page 46.

Helxine. See Soleirolia

HEMEROCALLIS. Daylily. Perennial with fleshy roots. Deciduous or evergreen. Deciduous kinds very hardy in cold-winter areas. Striking display of lilylike flowers may last from spring to fall if you choose varieties carefully. *Culture:* Zones A–H, 3–10; either sun or part shade (in hot-test areas flowers fade or burn in full sun); no foot traffic; either small or large areas; fast growing; takes almost any soil; nearly pest free. Set nursery plants or divisions 12–18 inches apart; divide old clumps in late fall or early spring. Water well during bloom season. Feed with complete fertilizer in spring before flower stalks emerge, again in summer after main bloom is finished. *Foliage and flowers:* Grassy clumps of sword-shaped leaves arch at top. Individual plants resemble young corn. Varieties available in various sizes of plant, flower, stalk. Foliage 12–36 inches tall with open or branched flower clusters held well above foliage on bare stems ranging from 2–5 feet, depending on variety. Flowers range from yellow to orange, rust red, burgundy shades, pale pink, vermilion, buff apricot, creamy white, bicolored, or even creamy green. Some varieties bloom both spring and fall, others only once in spring to summer.

HERNIARIA glabra. Green carpet, rupture wort. Evergreen perennial. Fine-textured, mosslike plants with tiny leaves best in small areas—rock gardens, parking strips, between stepping stones. Easy to confine. *Culture:* Zones A–H, 5–10; either sun or shade; endures occasional traffic; fast growing. Set nursery plants 12 inches apart, closer for fast cover. *Foliage and flowers:* Trailing plants 2–3 inches tall, spread in circular patches until they touch. Tiny, crowded, bright green leaves less than ¼ inch long turn bronzy green in cold weather. Insignificant small greenish flowers.

HIPPOCREPIS comosa. Perennial. Good bank cover (roots bind soil) or small-scale lawn substitute. *Culture:* Zones D–H, 8–10; full sun; takes light foot traffic; best in small to medium-size areas; fast growing; tolerates poor, dry soil, but has better appearance with good soil, adequate water. Set nursery plants 12 inches apart. Mow plantings just after blooms fade. *Foliage and flowers:* Plants form mats 3 inches high, to 3 feet across. Medium green leaves divided into many tiny leaflets. Produces clusters of small, golden, sweet pealike flowers in spring; may repeat in summer.

HOSTA (Funkia). Plantain lily. Lush, leafy, perennial cover for light or deep-shaded areas. Handsome large leaves carried at ends of slim leaf stalks form clumps of overlapping foliage. Will take sun, if heat not too intense or if atmospheric humidity high. Foliage dies back in winter. None of the hostas take foot traffic. Specialists list many species, named varieties with fancy leaves at fancy prices. The hostas mentioned here are more available in general nursery trade. See photos on pages 50, 75.

H. decorata (*H.* 'Thomas Hogg'). *Culture:* Zones A–D, F, G, 4–10; best in partial to full shade, can take some sun; no foot traffic; best in small to medium-size areas; fast growing; must have regular water; mulch heavily to maintain moisture and keep mud from splashing on leaves. Slugs and snails can quickly disfigure foliage; bait for them as often as necessary. Set nursery plants 12–18 inches apart. *Foliage and flowers:* Plants to 1 foot tall with oval, 6-inch leaves, green with white margins. Lavender 2-inch flowers in summer on 2-foot stems.

H. 'Honeybells'. *Culture:* Same as *H. decorata*. *Foliage and flowers:* Grass-green leaves to 10 inches long, 7 inches wide; foliage mounds to 2 feet high. Fragrant flowers in shades of lilac on 3-foot stems.

H. lancifolia (*H. japonica*). Narrow-leafed plantain lily. *Culture:* Same as *H. decorata*. *Foliage and flowers:* Dark green, narrow, 6-inch-long leaves taper into the long leaf stalk; foliage mounds to about 20 inches. Two-inch lilac or pale lavender flowers on 2-foot stems in summer.

H. plantaginea (*H. grandiflora, H. subcordata*). Fragrant plantain lily. *Culture:* Same as *H. decorata*. *Foliage and flowers:* Leaves oval to heart-shaped, bright green, to 10 inches long; foliage mounds to 12–18 inches high. White flowers, 4–5 inches long on 2-foot stems in summer.

H. sieboldiana (*H. glauca*). *Culture:* Same as *H. decorata*. *Foliage and flowers:* Blue green leaves with heavy ribbing, oval to heart-shaped, 10–15 inches long; foliage mounds to about 12 inches. Slender, pale lilac flowers nestle among leaves in summer.

H. undulata (*H. media picta, H. variegata*). Wavy-leafed plantain lily. *Culture:* Same as *H. decorata*. *Foliage and flowers:* Wavy-margined, oval, green and white leaves, 6–8 inches long; foliage mounds to about 18 inches. Pale lavender flowers on 3-foot stalks in summer.

H. ventricosa (*H. caerulea*). Blue plantain lily. *Culture:* Same as *H. decorata*. *Foliage and flowers:* Broad, deep green leaves to 9 inches long with prominent ribs; foliage mounds from 18–24 inches high. Violet blue flowers on 3-foot stems in summer.

Hummingbird flower. See Zauschneria

HYPERICUM calycinum. Creeping St. Johnswort, Aaron's beard. Evergreen to semi-evergreen shrub. Tidy appearing, tough plant that will take sun or shade, good or poor soil, competition from tree roots, some drought. Spreads by underground stems, can be invasive unless confined by wood, concrete, or metal barrier that extends several inches below soil surface. *Culture:* Zones B–H, 6–10; full sun or partial shade; no foot traffic (you can wade through without damage); medium to large areas; fast growing; any type soil. Set nursery plants or rooted stems 18 inches apart. Mow or cut back every 2–3 years during dormant season to keep even. *Foliage and flowers:* Medium green, 4-inch leaves in sun, yellow green in shade. Erect dense stems to 12 inches tall. Bright yellow, 3-inch flowers in summer. See photos on page 75.

IBERIS sempervirens. Evergreen candytuft. Perennial. Long-stemmed flower clusters make good cut flowers. *Culture:* Zones A–H, 4–10; full sun or partial shade; no foot traffic; small to medium-size areas; fast growing. Set nursery plants 9–12 inches apart (further apart for 'Purity' and 'Snowflake', see below). Shear lightly after bloom to encourage new growth. *Foliage and flowers:* Tiny dark green leaves on 8–18-inch-tall stems, spreading to 18 inches. White clusters of tiny flowers from early spring to June; may bloom as early as November in mild climates. Lower, more compact forms include 'Little Gem', 4–6 inches tall; 'Purity', 6–12 inches tall, wide spreading; 'Snowflake', 4–12 inches high, 1½–3 feet across with broader, more leathery leaves, larger flowers on shorter stems. See photo on page 76.

ICE PLANT. Succulent perennials once classified as *Mesembryanthemum* are now grouped under several different names. Fat-leafed plant common along California beaches and highways is *Carpobrotus*. Other good ground covers for mild-winter areas are *Cephalophyllum, Delosperma, Drosanthemum, Lampranthus,* and *Malephora.* Some produce such vivid flower color they seem artificial and overwhelming in the garden. Following are individual descriptions. See photos on pages 49, 64, 76.

CARPOBROTUS. Sea fig. *Culture:* Zones E (warmer parts)–H, 9, 10; full sun; no foot traffic; good in large areas; fast growing; withstands some drought. Set nursery plants or cuttings 18–24 inches apart. Poor for steep slopes as weight of plant can pull it from soil. *Foliage and flowers:* C. chilensis (California beach plant) has fat, three-sided, straight leaves, some with reddish tones. Fairly sparse, rosy purple flowers in summer. C. edulis has fat curved leaves, pale yellow to rose flowers.

CEPHALOPHYLLUM 'Red Spike'. (Often sold as *Cylindrophyllum speciosum*). *Culture:* Zones D, E (all but coldest), F–H, 9, 10; full sun; no foot traffic; medium-size areas; fast growing; withstands some drought. Set nursery plants 6–12 inches apart. *Foliage and flowers:* Clumping plant 3–5 inches tall, spreading to 15–18 inches. Bronzy red leaves point straight up. Bright, cerise red, 2-inch flowers profuse in winter, light in other seasons.

DELOSPERMA 'Alba'. *Culture:* Zones E (warmest parts)–H, 9, 10; full sun; no foot traffic; small to medium-size areas; fast growing. Set nursery plants 12 inches apart. Good for holding soil on fairly steep banks. *Foliage and flowers:* Dwarf, spreading; roots along stems. Small fleshy leaves have good green color. Small white flowers, not showy.

DROSANTHEMUM. *Culture:* Zones F–H, 9, 10; full sun; no foot traffic; medium to large areas; fast growing; tolerates poor soils. Set nursery plants 12–18 inches apart. Good plant to control erosion on steep slopes. Flowers attract bees. *Foliage and flowers:* Trailing, rooting stems bear dense, small, dark green leaves covered with sparkling fleshy dots. Plant reaches 6 inches tall, spreads wide. D. floribundum has ¾-inch pink flowers in spring, early summer. D. hispidum has solid carpet of 1-inch, purple flowers in spring, early summer.

LAMPRANTHUS. *Culture:* Zones F–H, 9, 10; full sun; no foot traffic; medium to large areas; fast growing. Set nursery plants 12–18 inches apart. Cut back lightly after bloom fades to remove fruit capsules, encourage new growth. *Foliage and flowers:* L. aurantiacus has gray green, 3-sided leaves 1 inch long. Orange, 2-inch-wide flowers February–May. Varieties include 'Glaucus', yellow flowers; 'Sunman', gold yellow flowers. L. filicaulis has thin creeping stems, fine-textured foliage; spreads slowly to form 3-inch-deep mats. Small, pink

(Continued on page 79)

HYPERICUM calycinum

Easy-to-grow, spreading shrub will thrive in sun or shade, good or poor soil; can stand competition from tree roots, some drought. Hypericum mixed with Hedera helix grows down steep slope (left). Flowers (below) bloom throughout summer. (See page 74.)

HOSTA

These lush, handsome plants form clumps of overlapping leaves in shady areas. Hosta sieboldiana (left) has large, blue green, heavily ribbed leaves. Slender flowers in pale lilac color appear in summer. Hosta decorata (above) displays green leaves variegated with silvery white margins. Lavender flowers bloom in summer on 2-foot stalks. (See pages 73–74.)

ICE PLANT

Good ground covers for mild-winter areas. Most varieties produce such vivid flower color in winter, spring, early summer that they seem almost artificial. Spring-blooming Lampranthus spectabilis (right) is used as a slope stabilizer in this garden. Also useful in coastal gardens (below), lampranthus thrives on salt air, sandy soil. (See pages 74, 79.)

JUNIPERUS horizontalis 'Bar Harbor'
Ground-hugging shrub can spread up to 10 feet across, but stays 12 inches tall. Foliage is bluish green. (See page 79.)

IBERIS sempervirens
White clusters of tiny flowers from early spring to June make this cover a favorite. Flowers may appear in November in mild areas. (See page 74.)

LANTANA

In mild climates, these shrubby ground covers (left) are planted for their profuse flower display. Blooms may be orange, yellow, lavender, pink, white, purple; some forms come in color combinations. Close-up (below) shows toothed, dark green foliage, flowers. (See page 79.)

LAURENTIA fluviatilis

Ground-hugging, creeping perennial with dense, tiny, oval leaves makes a good lawn substitute; it can handle light foot traffic. In spring and summer, bluish white flowers dot the green carpet (below left). In close-up (below right), fingertips contrast with tiny star-shaped blooms. (See page 80.)

LIRIOPE muscari

Dark green, grassy clumps make excellent borders, edgings. In summer, flower spikes 6 to 8 inches long appear on stems up to 12 inches, followed by sparse, shiny, black fruit. Flower clusters may be obscured among leaves. (See page 80.)

LYSIMACHIA nummularia

For damp, shaded areas, natural woodsy settings. Trailing plant with roundish light green leaves forms a low mat. In summer, yellow flowers put on quite a show. (See page 80.)

LONICERA japonica 'Halliana'

Rampant, aggressive vine for covering banks and large, out-of-the-way areas; good erosion control. Branches with spaced pairs of deep green leaves can reach 15 feet long. White tubular flowers in pairs turn yellow, have strong fragrance. (See page 80.)

spring flowers. *L. productus* has gray green, fleshy bronze-tipped leaves. One-inch purple flowers heavy in winter, spring. *L. spectabilis* is 12 inches tall, to 2 feet wide. Gray green foliage covered with carpet of pink, rose pink, red, or purple flowers March–May.

MALEPHORA (*Hymenocyclus*). *Culture:* Zones E (all but coldest)–H, 9, 10; full sun; no foot traffic; medium to large areas; fast growing. Set nursery plants 12–18 inches apart. *M. crocea* good bank cover. *Foliage and flowers:* *M. crocea* has gray green foliage on trailing plants. Reddish yellow or salmon flowers bloom sparsely all year, more heavily in spring. *M. luteola* (Zones F–H, 9, 10) has gray green foliage, sparse yellow bloom.

Indian mock strawberry. See Duchesnea

Inside-out flower. See Vancouveria

Irish moss. See Sagina

Isotoma. See Laurentia

Ivy. See Hedera

Ivy geranium. See Pelargonium

J

Japanese spurge. See Pachysandra

Jasmine. See Jasminum

JASMINUM polyanthum. Jasmine. For another popular ground cover called star jasmine, see *Trachelospermum*, page 90. For warm climates only. *Culture:* Zones D (all but coldest), E (warmest), F–H, 8–10; full sun; no foot traffic; medium to large areas; fast growing. Set nursery plants 10 feet apart. Cut back any tangled growth each spring. Needs regular watering in summer. *Foliage and flowers:* Evergreen vine with finely divided leaflets; can reach 20 feet long. Dense clusters of fragrant flowers, white inside, rose outside, bloom February–July in warm climates, from April in cooler areas.

Jewel mint of Corsica. See Mentha

Juniper. See Juniperus

JUNIPERUS. Juniper. Evergreen coniferous shrubs with fleshy berrylike cones on female plants. Junipers used as ground covers range from flat mats a few inches high to 3-foot-high shrubs. Foliage colors range from silvery blue to yellowish green and var-

iegated. Foliage may be needlelike, scalelike, or both on the same plant, depending on the species or variety. Most plants listed below stay under 12 inches high. See photos on pages 46, 47, 76.

J. chinensis sargentii (*J. sargentii, J. sargentii viridis*). *Culture:* Zones A–H, 3–10; full sun where summers are cool but will accept light shade; no foot traffic; good in medium to large areas; slow to moderate growth rate; any soil type, as long as it isn't constantly wet. Set nursery plants 5–6 feet apart; mulch to control weeds. *Foliage:* Gray green or green, feathery foliage on woody, ground hugging plant; 12 inches tall, to 10 feet across. Variety 'Glauca' has blue green foliage.

J. communis saxatilis (*J. c. montana, J. sibirica*). *Culture:* Same as *J. chinensis sargentii*. *Foliage:* Prostrate, trailing with variable gray or gray green foliage, 12 inches tall, 6–8 feet across. Branch tips turn up.

J. conferta. Shore juniper. Good seashore plant; can take heat if grown in moist, well-drained soil. *Culture:* Same as *J. chinensis sargentii*. *Foliage:* Bright green, soft-needled foliage on prostrate plant to 8 feet across.

J. horizontalis, 'Bar Harbor'. Fast growing. *J. h.* 'Venusta' similar. *Culture:* Same as *J. chinensis sargentii*. *Foliage:* Feathery blue gray foliage turns plum color in cold weather. Ground hugging, up to 12 inches high, to 10 feet across.

J. h. 'Douglasii'. Waukegan juniper. *Culture:* Same as *J. chinensis sargentii*. *Foliage:* Steel blue foliage turns purplish in fall; new growth rich green. Trailing to 10 feet across, no more than 1 foot high.

J. h. 'Webberi'. *Culture:* Same as *J. chinensis sargentii*. *Foliage:* Heavy, bluish green, matlike foliage spreads to 8 feet but not over 1 foot high.

J. h. 'Wiltonii'. (*J. h.* 'Blue Rug'). Blue carpet juniper. *Culture:* Same as *J. chinensis sargentii*. *Foliage:* Lowest juniper, 4 inches tall, to 8–10 feet across. Intense silver blue foliage; long trailing branches.

J. sabina 'Buffalo'. *Culture:* Same as *J. chinensis sargentii*. *Foliage:* Feathery bright green foliage; grows to 1 foot high and spreads to 8 feet.

J. s. 'Tamariscifolia'. Tamarix juniper, Tam. *Culture:* Same as *J. chinensis sargentii*. *Foliage:* Blue green, very dense foliage, 18 inches tall, spreads symmetrically to 20 feet.

J. scopulorum 'White's Silver King'. *Culture:* Same as *J. chinensis sargentii*. *Foliage:* Pale silver blue foliage on dense, spreading plant, 10 inches tall, 6–8 feet across.

K

Kenilworth ivy. See Cymbalaria

Kew broom. See Cytisus

Kinnikinnick. See Arctostaphylos

Knotweed. See Polygonum

Korean grass. See Zoysia

L

Lampranthus. See Ice plant

LANTANA. Woody, trailing or spreading shrubs for fairly mild climates. Planted for profuse flower display, generally in orange, yellow, lavender, pink, white, purple, and some combined forms. Small black berries follow flowers. Crushed foliage has odd odor. Ground cover lantanas in nurseries are crosses between shrubby *L. camara* and trailing *L. montevidensis* (*L. sellowiana*). The latter species may also be available—lilac rosy flowers on a low, trailing plant that can spread to 6 feet across; 'Velutina White', a white flowered form. *Culture:* Zones E (warmest parts), F–H, 10; full sun, plants subject to mildew in shade or continual overcast; no foot traffic; small or large areas; fast growing; good in any soil. Set plants 3 feet apart; cut back in spring to remove any excessively woody growth. Water deeply and infrequently. Overfertilizing cuts down on bloom. *Foliage and flowers:* Dark green, coarse, toothed leaves to 1 inch long may turn red or purplish in cool weather. Blooms all year in frost-free areas. Flower color depends on variety: 'Carnival' ('Dwarf Carnival'), to 2 feet tall, 4 feet wide—pink, yellow, crimson, lavender; 'Confetti', to 3 feet tall, 8 feet wide—yellow, pink, purple; 'Cream Carpet', to 3 feet tall, 8 feet wide—cream with bright yellow throat; 'Gold Mound', to 2 feet tall, 6 feet wide—yellow orange; 'Kathleen', to 2 feet tall, 6 feet wide—blend of soft rose and gold; 'Pink Frolic', to 3 feet tall, 8 feet wide—pink and yellow; 'Spreading Sunset', to 3 feet tall, 8 feet wide—vivid orange red; 'Spreading Sunshine', to 3 feet tall, 8 feet wide—yellow; 'Sunburst', to 3 feet tall, 8 feet wide—golden yellow; 'Tangerine', to 3 feet tall, 8 feet wide—burnt orange. See photos on page 77.

LATHYRUS latifolius. Perennial sweet pea for a naturalistic appearing cover on banks, rugged ground. *Culture:* Zones A–H, 4–10; full sun; no foot traffic; good in medium-size areas; fast growing. Sow seed heavily or set nursery plants 2 feet apart. *Foliage and flowers:* Blue green foliage consisting of 4-inch leaflets on vines to 9 feet long. Not a dense cover. Reddish, red violet, rose, or white flowers resemble 1½-inch sweet peas in clusters. If seed pods are removed, flowers will bloom June–September.

LAURENTIA fluviatilis (*Isotoma fluviatilis*). Blue star creeper. Creeping perennial with tiny star-shaped flowers. *Culture:* Zones B, D, F–H, may not be successful east of the Rockies; best in light shade, but will take sun if given plenty of water; will take some foot traffic, best for small areas; fast growing; likes loose, fast-draining soil. Set nursery plants 6–12 inches apart. *Foliage and flowers:* Dense, tiny, oval leaves 2–3-inch plants that resemble baby's tears (see *Soleirolia*, page 89). Tiny starlike blue or white flowers in spring, summer, but flowers can appear at other times. See photos on pages 45 and 77.

Lily-of-the-valley. See Convallaria

Lingonberry. See Vaccinium

Lippia. See Phyla

LIRIOPE. Flowering, grassy perennials related to the lily. Some spread by underground runners; others form clumps. See photos on pages 50, 78.

L. muscari (often sold as 'Big Blue'). Big blue lily turf. *Culture:* Zones B(all but coldest), C, D, E (warmest), F–H, 6–10; full sun, partial shade in hot-summer areas; no foot traffic; best in small areas; fast growing. Set divisions or nursery plants 8–12 inches apart in well-drained soil; keep moist. If planting gets ragged and brown, cut back old foliage after new leaves appear. Extended frost will turn foliage yellow; it recovers slowly. Divide in early spring. Bait for slugs and snails. *Foliage and flowers:* Large, loose clumps to 18 inches high with arching dark green leaves to 2 feet long by ½ inch wide; plant does not spread by underground stems. Flower spikes 6–8 inches long on stems to 12 inches may be partly hidden among leaves in older plants. Dark violet buds and flowers followed by sparse, black, shiny fruit. Dense bloom resembles grape hyacinth. Variety 'Majestic' is taller than most; flowers stand well above leaves. 'Silvery Sunproof' has

open erect leaves with gold stripes that turn white as leaves mature; lilac flowers rise above leaves, need full shade in heat. 'Variegata' (may be sold as *Ophiopogon jaburan* 'Variegata') does best in part shade; new leaves are green with yellow edges, becoming dark green in second year; violet flowers rise above foliage.

L. spicata. Creeping lily turf. Hardy in cold areas but looks shabby in winter. Should be mowed every year just before spring growth starts. *Culture:* Zones A–H, 4–10; otherwise, same as *L. muscari*. *Foliage and flowers:* Dense clumps, 8–9 inches high spread by underground stems; leaves ½ inch across, softer and less upright than *L. muscari*. Pale lilac to white flowers on spikes barely taller than leaves.

Little Sur manzanita. See Arctostaphylos

Longleaf mahonia. See Mahonia

Longspur epimedium. See Epimedium

LONICERA japonica 'Halliana'. Hall's Japanese honeysuckle. Rampant growing, aggressive vine for covering banks, large out-of-the-way areas, or for erosion control. Should be sheared back to ground annually in late winter to prevent buildup of dead stems that can become a fire hazard. *Culture:* Zones A(all but coldest)–H, 5–10; full sun or partial shade; no foot traffic; best in large areas; tolerates most soils. Deciduous in cold climates. Set nursery plants or cuttings 3 feet apart. Fairly drought tolerant when established. *Foliage and flowers:* Branches to 15 feet long with spaced pairs of 3-inch, oval, deep green leaves. White tubular flowers in pairs turn yellow, strong evening fragrance, attract bees, birds. See photo on page 78.

LOTUS. Two species have somewhat different functions as ground covers: one is a trailing ground cover, the other a possible lawn substitute.

L. berthelotii. Parrot's beak. Perennial. *Culture:* Zones F–H, 10; full sun to part shade; no foot traffic; best in small to medium-size areas; fast growing; must have good drainage, some summer water. Set nursery plants 24 inches apart. Cut back occasionally to keep bushy. *Foliage and flowers:* Attractive, feathery, silver gray leaves thickly cover stems 2–3 feet long. Profuse, narrow, 1-inch, scarlet blossoms in June–July.

L. corniculatus. Birdsfoot trefoil. Perennial. *Culture:* Zones B–H, 6–10; full sun; will take some foot traffic; good in small or large areas; fast

growing; needs ample water in dry hot-summer areas, as it will die in drought conditions. Must have water for permanent lawn cover. Mow occasionally to about 2 inches tall, more frequently if used as lawn substitute, about half as frequently if used as lawn. Sow seed on prepared ground for use as lawn, or set plants 6 inches apart if used as ordinary ground cover. Will reseed and resprout each year. *Foliage and flowers:* Flat round mats of dark green, cloverlike foliage. Semievergreen through winter in mild areas; goes dormant in coldest areas. Yellow flowers in summer, fall. Seed pods at top of flower stem spread like a bird's foot, hence common name.

LYSIMACHIA nummularia. Creeping Jennie, moneywort. Perennial. For damp, shady areas on low-lying ground, near streams, or in light shade where it can be well watered. Best in natural woodsy settings. *Culture:* Zones A–D, F–H, 4–10; partial or full shade; no foot traffic; good in small to medium-size areas; fast growing; must have moist soil. Set nursery plants or rooted segments 12–18 inches apart. *Foliage and flowers:* Long trailing runners to 2 feet that root at joints. Roundish, 1-inch-long, light green leaves form a mat. One-inch-wide yellow flowers form singly in leaf joints in summer. See photos on pages 50, 78.

MAHONIA. Evergreen, spiny-leafed western native. Drought resistant.

M. nervosa. Longleaf mahonia. *Culture:* Zones A(all but coldest)–D, F, 6–9; best in shade, very compact in sunny cooler areas; no foot traffic; good in medium-size areas; slow to moderate growth rate; spreads by underground stems. Set nursery plants 12 inches apart. *Foliage, flowers, and fruit:* Generally a low shrub to 2 feet tall. Cut back taller growth to keep low. Leaves 10–18 inches long, with 7–21 glossy, bristle-toothed, green leaflets, cluster at stem tips. Upright 6-inch clusters of yellow flowers April–June, followed by edible blue berries.

M. repens. Creeping mahonia. *Culture:* Zones A–G, 6–9; sun or partial shade; no foot traffic; good in medium-size areas; slow to moderate growth rate. Set nursery plants 2 feet apart. *Foliage, flowers, and fruit:* Plant creeps by underground stems to 3 feet tall, spreading wide. Dull, blue green leaves, divided into 3–7 spiny leaflets, turn bronze in winter. Yellow flower spikes April–June, followed by blue berries.

Malephora. See Ice plant

Manzanita. See Arctostaphylos

Mattress vine. See Muehlenbeckia

MAZUS reptans. Small-scale perennial cover for small areas, spaces between steppingstones. Freezes in cold winters, but resprouts; is evergreen in mild areas. *Culture:* Zones A–H, 4–10; good in sun or very light shade; takes very light foot traffic; fast growing; needs rich moist soil. Set nursery plants 6 inches apart. *Foliage and flowers:* Slender creeping stems root along ground, send up leafy branches 1–2 inches tall. Bright green narrow leaves to 1 inch long, slightly toothed. Purple blue flowers with white and yellow markings, ¾ inch across in small clusters, bloom spring, early summer.

MENTHA requienii. Jewel mint of Corsica. Perennial. Tiny-leafed low creeper has pleasant minty fragrance when walked on. Freezes in cold weather, but resprouts if ground is not frozen. Use it among steppingstones or on earth-cut steps for fragrance. Can be invasive. *Culture:* Zones B (all but coldest), D, E (warmer areas), F–H, 6–10; good in sun or light shade; can withstand very light traffic; best in small areas; fairly fast growing; needs moisture. Set nursery plants or divisions 6 inches apart. *Foliage and flowers:* Mat of tiny, round, ½-inch-tall bright green leaves gives mossy effect. Tiny purple flowers in summer.

Mondo grass. See Ophiopogon

Moneywort. See Lysimachia

Morning glory. See Convolvulus

Moss pink. See Phlox

MUEHLENBECKIA. Wire vine. Unusual evergreen vine with thin wiry stems. Requires routine summer watering. Flowers insignificant. See photo on page 83.

M. axillaris (M. nana). Creeping wire vine. *Culture:* Zones A (warmest)–D, F, H, 5–10; full sun to medium shade; will take light foot traffic; best in small areas; moderate growth rate. Deciduous where winter chill is pronounced. Set plants 6–12

inches apart. *Foliage:* Small creeping plant 2–4 inches tall, or mounding up to 1 foot. Spreads by underground stems. Glossy, dark green to bronzy, closely spaced leaves ⅛ inch long.

M. complexa. Mattress vine, wire vine. *Culture:* Zones D, F–H, 8–10; full sun; no foot traffic; good in large areas; moderate to fast growth rate. Set plants 3 feet apart. Good for beach plantings, cut banks, or other rugged areas away from cultivated garden. *Foliage:* Dense tangle of tough black or brown stems with variable leaves to ¾ inch long.

MYOPORUM parvifolium. Neat shrubby cover especially good along coast (it tolerates salt spray, sandy soil) and where summers are cool. *Culture:* Zones D (warmest areas), F–H, 9, 10; full sun; no foot traffic; good in medium to large areas; fast growing; moderately drought tolerant; but best with some summer water. Set nursery plants 3–6 feet apart; will fill in within 6 months. Branch stems root wherever they touch moist soil. *Foliage, flowers, and fruit:* Plants to 3 inches tall, 9 feet across, densely covered with bright green, oval leaves to 1 inch long. Bell-shaped, ½-inch, white flowers in summer, followed by purple berries.

MYOSOTIS scorpioides. Forget-me-not. Perennial similar to the old-fashioned familiar annual, but lower growing. Pleasant effect under trees. Dies back in winter; roots survive from year to year. *Culture:* Zones A–H, 4–10; best in full or partial shade; no foot traffic; limit to small areas; fast growing; likes ample moisture. Set nursery plants 6–12 inches apart or sow seed. *Foliage and flowers:* Plants 6–10 inches tall with narrow, bright green, shiny, oblong leaves to 2 inches long. Sprays of small, delicate, ¼-inch blue flowers with white, yellow, or pink centers over a long blooming season, in late spring, summer.

Myrtle. See Vinca

N

Natal plum. See Carissa grandiflora

NEPETA faassenii. Catmint. Perennial closely related to catnip. *Culture:* Zones A–H, 4–10; either sun or shade; withstands light traffic; use in me-

dium-size areas; fast growing. Set nursery plants 12–18 inches apart; shear after flowers fade to encourage second bloom. *Foliage and flowers:* Soft, gray green mounds to 2 feet tall; rather narrow, 1½-inch-long leaves with pleasant odor. Loose spikes of lavender blue flowers in summer.

NIEREMBERGIA Perennial. Tubular flowers flaring into saucerlike or bell-like cup. See photos on pages 46, 83.

N. hippomanica violacea (N. h. caerulea). Dwarf cup flower. *Culture:* Zones D–H, 7–10; full sun, very light shade in hot-summer areas; no foot traffic; good in small to medium-size areas; moderate growth rate. Set plants 6–12 inches apart. Give moderate amounts of water. *Foliage and flowers:* Much-branched, mounding plant to 6–12 inches high. Stiff, very narrow, ½-⅔-inch-long leaves. Blue to violet bell-like flowers all summer. Trimming back to induce new growth seems to lengthen life. Good edging plant for semishade in desert regions. Variety 'Purple Robe' readily available.

N. repens (N. rivularis). White cup. *Culture:* Zones B (all but coldest), D, F–H, 7–10; otherwise same as N. hippomanica violacea. *Foliage and flowers:* Prostrate mat of bright green, rather stiff leaves to ⅔ inch long. White, bell-like flowers 1 inch wide all summer.

O

OPHIOPOGON japonicus. Mondo grass. Perennial. Grassy clumps of foliage and spikes of lilac flowers; similar to Liriope (see page 80). *Culture:* Zones B (all but coldest), C, D, E (warmest), F–H, 7–10; full sun, light shade in hot dry areas; no foot traffic; best in medium-size areas; slow to establish. Roots die at 10° F. Easy to divide. Set nursery plants or divisions 6–8 inches apart. If foliage becomes ratty, cut back in early spring before new growth begins. *Foliage and flowers:* Dense clumps spread by underground stems which are sometimes tuberlike. Dark green, ⅛-inch-wide leaves reach 12 inches long, form clumps of fountainlike foliage. Short spikes of lilac flowers. A black-leafed form, O. planiscapus 'Arabicus', forms tuft 8 inches high, a novelty in summer. Blue fruit. See photo on page 84.

Oregon oxalis. See Oxalis

ORIGANUM dictamnus (*Amaracus dictamnus*). Dittany of Crete. Perennial plant, an aromatic herb in the thyme-mint family. *Culture:* Zones D–H, 9, 10; full sun; no foot traffic; for small areas only; moderate growth; withstands drought, poor soil. Grow from nursery plants, rooted stems, or cuttings. Plant 12 inches apart, closer for faster cover. To encourage rooting, pin down stems. *Foliage and flowers:* Arching stems to 1 foot long bear pairs of roundish, fleshy, woolly, whitish gray green leaves that smell like thyme or marjoram. Odd-shaped pink to purplish flowers grow at branch tips late summer to fall, sprouting from hoplike head of purple bracts which last after flowers fade.

OSTEOSPERMUM fruticosum (*Dimorphotheca fruiticosa*). Trailing African daisy. Perennial. Very profuse bloom from fall to spring, scattered in summer. *Culture:* Zones D, F–H, 9, 10; full sun; no foot traffic; good in large areas; fast growing. Spreads rapidly by trailing, rooting stems. Set nursery plants 2 feet apart. Plants look best with moderate watering, good garden soil, though will stand drought, neglect when established. *Foliage and flowers:* Narrow, grayish green foliage on plants 6–12 inches tall. Daisies white with lavender backs and blue centers, or reddish violet with dark centers. Bloom is heaviest November–March, but intermittent all year. See photos on page 84.

OXALIS oregana. Redwood sorrel, Oregon oxalis. Perennial for deep shade in mild-winter, cool-summer regions. *Culture:* Zones B–D, F–H, not always successful east of the Rockies; full shade; no foot traffic; best in small or medium-size areas; fast growing; must have year-round moisture. Good companion for ferns. Set plants 6–12 inches apart, mulch. *Foliage and flowers:* Creeping roots send up large, velvety, medium green, cloverlike leaves to 4 inches wide on stems 2–10 inches high. Pink or white flowers veined with lavender are five-petaled, to 1 inch across, bloom in spring, sometimes again in fall. See photo on page 84.

PACHYSANDRA terminalis. Japanese spurge. Perennial. Excellent choice for lush foliage in shady areas. *Culture:* Zones A–E (coldest parts), F, G (all but warmest), 5–9; full or part shade; no foot traffic; good in small to medium-size areas; fast growing; needs moist, rich, acid soil. Set plants 12 inches apart. *Foliage and flowers:* Underground runners send up stems to 10 inches in deep shade, 6 inches where there is filtered sun. Clusters of large dark green leaves to 4 inches long at tops of stems; forms dense cover. Small fluffy spikes of white flowers in summer, may be followed by white fruit. See photo on page 85.

Parrot's beak. See Lotus

PARTHENOCISSUS quinquefolia (*Ampelopsis quinquefolia*). Virginia creeper. Deciduous vine more frequently seen climbing walls, fences, or trees. *Culture:* Zones A–H, 3–10; full sun or partial shade; no foot traffic; good in medium to large areas; fast growing. Set plants 3 feet apart. Good on slopes; plant will attempt to climb any shrubs, trees, fences, or structures it encounters. *Foliage:* Large leaves with 5 separate leaflets, each to 6 inches long with saw-toothed edges. Spectacular orange to red fall foliage color.

PAXISTIMA canbyi. Ratstripper. Compact evergreen native of mountain regions of eastern United States. *Culture:* Zones A–E (coldest parts), F, G (all but warmest), 5–9; full sun near coast, partial shade elsewhere; no foot traffic; small or large areas; slow to moderate growth rate; needs moist soil. Set plants 12 inches apart. *Foliage:* Forms mat 9–12 inches tall with narrow leaves to 1 inch long, ¼ inch wide; green in summer, turning bronze in fall and winter. *P. myrsinites*, native to the West, grows almost twice as tall with somewhat larger leaves.

PELARGONIUM. Geranium. Pelargoniums are not true geraniums, which tend to be smaller, less showy plants (see page 72). Shrubby perennials. Ivy geranium common ground cover in warm regions. In mildest climates, you can experiment with some of the scented geraniums for ground cover. See photos on pages 49, 85.
  P. peltatum. Ivy geranium. *Culture:* Zones F, G (warmer parts), H, 9, 10; full sun; no foot traffic; good in small or large areas; fast growing. Set nursery plants 18–24 inches apart. If you plant cuttings, place 2 or 3 per planting hole 12 inches apart, in early fall; mulch and keep moist. Plants may need replacing in 3 or 4 years. *Foliage and flowers:* Succulent, glossy, bright green, ivylike leaves along trailing stems that reach 3 feet long. Showy clusters of single or double flowers in white, pink, rose, red, or lavender. Heaviest bloom in warmest months.
  P. tomentosum. Peppermint-scented geranium. *Culture:* Zones F, G (warmest parts), H, 9, 10; partial shade; no foot traffic; small or medium-size areas; fast growing. Set nursery plants 12–18 inches apart, or place several cuttings in planting holes 12 inches apart and keep moist. *Foliage and flowers:* Velvety, rounded and lobed silvery green leaves up to 5 inches across; crushed foliage has strong peppermint odor. Tiny white flowers in fluffy clusters pleasant but not showy. To experiment, try other scented pelargoniums. *P. fragrans*, nutmeg-scented, has tiny, rough, grayish leaves, profusion of tiny white flowers touched pink over long season; mounds to 12 inches or more. *P. odoratissimum*, apple-scented, 1–2-inch roundish, ruffled leaves, fluffy clusters of white flowers.

Periwinkle. See Vinca

PHLOX subulata. Moss pink. Evergreen perennial provides abundant bloom in wide range of colors. *Culture:* Zones A–F, 4–9; full sun; no foot traffic; good in small to medium-size areas; fast growing. Set plants 12–18 inches apart or sow seeds in spring. Prefers loose, not too rich soil. After flowering, shear back halfway. *Foliage and flowers:* Mats of stiff, needlelike, 6-inch-high foliage to ½–1 inch long; creeping stems. Abundant ¾-inch flowers in late spring or early summer ranging from white through pinks and rose, to lavender blue. See photo on page 48.

PHYLA nodiflora (*Lippia nodiflora*). Lippia. Old-fashioned perennial lawn substitute that attracts bees. If bees are objectionable, mow off flower tops. Goes dormant; is unattractive in winter. *Culture:* Zones D–H, 9, 10; full sun; takes some foot traffic; good in small to medium-size areas; fast growing. Set plants 2 feet apart in soil prepared for lawn, or set rooted stolons 12 inches apart. Mow, water, and fertilize regularly. Particularly useful in desert areas, but subject to nematodes. *Foliage and flowers:* Creeping flat mat with tiny gray green leaves. Small white or lilac flowers spring-fall. Form *rosea* has rose colored flowers; often sold as *Lippia repens*. See photo on page 85.

**NIEREMBERGIA
hippomanica violacea**
*Attractive, long-blooming
mat; fine cover for small
areas with full sun, good
soil. Plants have bright
green, rather stiff leaves,
bluish purple flowers;
white-flowered form also
available. (See page 81.)*

MUEHLENBECKIA complexa
*Unusual evergreen vine with thin, wiry
stems. Good for large areas, beach plantings, cut banks in full sun. Plant forms
a dense mat of tough black or brown stems
with variable, dark green leaves.
(See page 81.)*

OPHIOPOGON planiscapus 'Arabicus'
Black-leafed form of mondo grass makes fountain-like grassy clumps of foliage. Good for borders, edgings, mixed plantings. Pink flowers on spikes bloom in summer, are followed by fruit. (See page 81.)

OXALIS oregana
Perennial ground cover for deep-shaded, moist areas in mild-winter, cool-summer regions. Plant has large, velvety, medium green, cloverlike leaves up to 4 inches wide. Pink or white flowers with lavender veins bloom in spring, may repeat in fall. (See page 82.)

OSTEOSPERMUM fruticosum
Frequently planted in masses on large banks, along highways, osteo-spermum (right) is a popular trailing cover grown for its profuse fall-to-spring flowers. White backed with lavender or solid reddish violet daisylike flowers with dark centers (above) may appear sporadically in summer. (See page 82.)

PELARGONIUM peltatum
A fast-growing cover for warm, mild climates. Bright green, spreading foliage on trailing stems shows off clusters of single or double flowers in white, pink, red, or lavender. Heaviest bloom in warmest months. (See page 82.)

PACHYSANDRA terminalis
Excellent, lush foliage plant in shady areas with moist, rich, acid soil. Clusters of large, deep green leaves form a dense cover. Small spikes of fragrant white flowers in summer. Design: W. David Poot. (See page 82.)

PHYLA nodiflora
Old-fashioned perennial lawn substitute for sunny spots. Plant makes a creeping, flat, walkable mat with tiny gray green leaves. Small white or pink flowers in tight heads. (See page 82.)

POTENTILLA tabernaemontanii

Strawberrylike creeping plant (below) forms dense
cover that can be walked on. Flower color abundant
in spring, summer. Bright green, glossy foliage
(right) resembles strawberry leaves but has five
leaflets, bright yellow flowers in clusters.
(See page 87.)

POLYGONUM capitatum

An evergreen cover in mild-winter areas, polygonum is a tough, invasive, trailing plant best used
in out-of-the-way areas where roots can be confined.
Foliage opens green, turns pink with age. Tiny but
showy pink flowers in tight heads bloom most of
year. (See page 87.)

Piggy-back plant. See Tolmiea

Pink. See Dianthus

Plantain lily. See Hosta

Plumbago. See Ceratostigma

Point Reyes cearothus. See Ceanothus

POLYGONUM. Knotweed. Large family of plants with 2 tough perennial ground covers. Dies back in cold winters. See photos on pages 47, 86.

P. capitatum. Evergreen in mildest areas. *Culture:* Zones D, E (warmest parts), F–H, 7–10; good in sun or light shade; no foot traffic; use in small to medium-size areas; fast growing. Leaves discolor and die in temperatures below 28° F. Best in out-of-the-way areas or in confined spaces where invasive roots can be controlled. Reseeds itself. Set nursery plants 12 inches apart. *Foliage and flowers:* Trailing plants to 6 inches tall, spreading to 20 inches across. Leaves, 1½ inches long, open green, turn pink with age. Stems and tiny flowers in tight showy heads are pink. Blooms most of year.

P. cuspidatum compactum (*P. reynoutria*). *Culture:* Zones A–H, 4–10; otherwise, same as *P. capitatum*. Plants are taller, stiffer. Use on dry banks, garden fringes where can't invade choice plantings. Dies back in winter. Set nursery plants 2 feet apart. *Foliage and flowers:* Plants from 10–24 inches high, spreading widely by creeping roots. Stiff, wiry, red stems. Heart-shaped, pale green leaves to 6 inches long have red veins, turn red in fall. Dense showy clusters of flowers, red in bud, pink when open, in late summer.

Pork and beans. See Sedum

POTENTILLA. Cinquefoil. Perennial. Creeping ground covers are strawberrylike, but leaves have five leaflets. Form dense covers; bloom well. See photos on page 86.

P. cinerea. *Culture:* Zones A–F, 4–9; full sun or partial shade; takes some foot traffic; good in small to medium-size areas; moderate to rapid growth rate. Set nursery plants 12 inches apart; keep weeded until plants fill in. *Foliage and flowers:* Matted stems 2–4 inches tall. Gray hairy leaves are whitewoolly underneath, divided into 5 wedge-shaped leaflets toothed at tips. Abundant, pale yellow flowers in spring and early summer.

P. tabernaemontanii (*P. verna*). Spring cinquefoil. *Culture:* Zones A–H, 4–9; otherwise, same as *P. cinerea*. Stands more moisture, may turn

brown in cold winters. *Foliage and flowers:* Bright green glossy leaves with 5 leaflets. Plant reaches 6 inches tall. To keep even, mow occasionally to 2 inches high. Clusters of 3–5 bright yellow ¼-inch flowers abundant in spring, summer.

PRATIA angulata. Perennial. New Zealand plant with creeping stems. *Culture:* Zones B–H (may be killed or badly damaged in coldest winter areas), 7–10; full sun in cool climates, needs shade where summers are hot; no foot traffic; likes rich soil, abundant water. Plant 6–8 inches apart for fairly fast cover. *Foliage and flowers:* Stems root at joints to form dense, shiny dark green mats. Leaves roundish, ½ inch long, with a few teeth. Flowers white or bluish, nearly ¾ inch wide, on 2-inch stalks. Flowers oddly shaped. See photo on page 45.

PYRACANTHA. Firethorn. Evergreen. Prostrate varieties of familiar large shrubs make excellent barrier ground covers; occasionally will send up vertical shoots. All have small oval leaves, are thorny.

P. angustifolia 'Gnome'. *Culture:* Zones A (all but coldest)–H, 7–10; full sun; no foot traffic; good in medium-size areas; moderate to fast growth rate. Set plants 3 feet apart. Cut out or pin down any vertical growth. For best berry production, cut back branches that have produced berries to a side shoot in spring. *Foliage and fruit:* Prostrate and spreading; orange berries.

P. 'Red Elf'. *Culture:* Zones B–D, E (warmer parts)–H, 8–10; otherwise, same as *P. angustifolia* 'Gnome'. Set plants 2 feet apart. *Foliage and fruit:* Mounding dwarf plants, somewhat spreading, to 2 feet tall, 3–4 feet across. Red berries.

P. 'Ruby Mound'. *Culture:* Zones B–D, E (warmer parts)–H, 8–10; otherwise, same as *P. angustifolia* 'Gnome'. Set plants 2 feet apart. *Foliage and fruit:* Mounding, to 1½ feet tall, 3 feet across. Red berries.

P. 'Santa Cruz' (*P.* 'Santa Cruz Prostrata'). *Culture:* Zones B–H, 8–10; otherwise, same as *P. angustifolia* 'Gnome'. Set nursery plants 4–5 feet apart. *Foliage and fruit:* Branching and spreading from base; easily kept below 3 feet. Red berries.

P. 'Walderi' (*P.* 'Walderi Prostrata'). *Culture:* Zones A (warmest parts)–H, 7–10; otherwise, same as *P. angustifolia* 'Gnome'. Set nursery plants 4–5 feet apart. *Foliage and fruit:* Low (to 18 inches), wide growth; red berries.

RANUNCULUS repens 'Pleniflorus'. Creeping buttercup. Vigorous spreading perennial for moist shady areas. Deciduous, resprouting from roots. *Culture:* Zones A–H, 4–9; filtered to full shade; no foot traffic; good in medium to large areas; fast growing; can be invasive; needs ample moisture. Set nursery plants 12–18 inches apart. *Foliage and flowers:* Glossy, roundish, deeply cut, toothed leaves densely sprouting from creeping stems several feet long that root as they creep. Very showy, shiny, double, button-shaped, yellow flowers to 1 inch across in spring.

Ratstripper. See Paxistima

Redwood sorrel. See Oxalis

RIBES viburnifolium. Catalina perfume, evergreen currant. Evergreen shrub that stays low, spreads wide. *Culture:* Zones D, F–H, 4–10; sun on coast, partial shade inland (foliage yellows in hot sun); no foot traffic; good in medium to large areas; moderate growth rate. Drought resistant when established. Set plants 3 feet apart. Prune out upright growth to keep low. Excellent high ground cover under native oaks where heavy watering undesirable. *Foliage and flowers:* Shrubby plants reach up to 3 feet tall, may spread to 12 feet. Arching or trailing, wine red stems may root where they touch moist soil. Leathery, roundish, dark green leaves to 1 inch across emit turpentinelike fragrance when moist or crushed. Light pink to purplish flowers are small in short upright clusters February–April, followed by red berries.

Rock cotoneaster. See Cotoneaster

Rockrose. See Cistus

Rockspray cotoneaster. See Cotoneaster

ROSA. Rose. Ground cover roses long-caned, heavy flowering, require pinning down of canes. Both evergreen and deciduous kinds. Best in large areas at garden edge where very long canes have room.

R. banksiae. Lady Banks' rose. *Culture:* Zones B–H, 7–10; full sun; no foot traffic; good in large areas; fast growing. Set plants 8 feet apart; pin down canes that grow upward. *Foliage and flowers:* Evergreen thornless canes to 20 feet long with glossy leaves, deciduous in cold-winter areas. Clusters of small yellow or white flowers late spring to midsummer depending on climate. Variety 'Alba Plena' has violet-scented white bloom; 'Lutea' double bloom with no scent.

R. bracteata 'Mermaid'. Mermaid rose. *Culture:* Zones B–H, 7–10; otherwise, same as *R. banksiae.* Disease resistant. *Foliage and flowers:* Evergreen or semi-evergreen, thorny canes to 30 feet long with glossy, dark green leaves. Creamy yellow, lightly fragrant, large single flowers to 5 inches across, in summer, fall, sparse into winter in mildest areas.

R. wichuraiana. Memorial rose. *Culture:* Zones A–H, 6–10; otherwise, same as *R. banksiae.* Will grow in relatively poor soil. *Foliage and flowers:* Shiny, dark green leaves composed of 7–9 leaflets, evergreen or partially evergreen; prostrate stems to 12 feet long will root where they touch moist soil. White, 2-inch, single flowers in clusters of 6–10 in midsummer. The hybrid 'Max Graf' has trailing stems and handsome glossy foliage; the 2–3-inch single pink flowers are produced over a long period in late spring.

Rose. See Rosa

Rosemary. See Rosmarinus

ROSMARINUS officinalis. Rosemary. Evergreen prostrate kinds produce masses of tiny blue flowers in mild climates in winter and early spring. Bees love them. Use foliage for sachets, cooking. *Culture:* Zones B–H, 7–9; full sun; no foot traffic; small or large areas; slow to start, then moderate growth rate. Best if it can grow naturally; pruned edges spoil casual layered effect. Set plants 2 feet apart. Will grow in poor soil if it has good drainage. Once established, needs some water in desert areas, little or no water elsewhere. *Foliage and flowers:* Fine needlelike leaves, dark green above, grayish beneath. Blue or blue violet flowers most of winter. Varieties include 'Collingwood Ingram' (*R. ingramii*), to 2½ feet tall by 4 feet wide, bright blue violet flowers; 'Lockwood de Forest', to 2 feet tall, 8 feet across, with blue flowers; 'Prostratus', to 2 feet tall, 8 feet across, blue to blue violet flowers. Will trail downward as curtain over banks or walls. See photos on pages 51, 91.

Rupture wort. See Herniaria

RUSCUS hypoglossum. Butcher's broom. Evergreen oddity for small-scale cover. *Culture:* Zones B–H, 8–

10; best in shade, will take some sun except in hot desert areas; no foot traffic; best in small areas; moderate to rapid growth rate. Set plants 2 feet apart. *Foliage and flowers:* Tough, narrow "leaves" are really flattened stems to 4 inches long, 1½ inches wide, glossy green, not spine-tipped. Plant grows to 1½ feet high and spreads by underground stems. Tiny, greenish white flowers bloom on "leaf" surface. If you have planted both male and female plants, marble-size, red or yellow berries should follow flowers.

S

SAGINA subulata. Irish moss, Scotch moss. Perennial. Two different plants, both frequently sold as *Sagina.* The other plant is *Arenaria verna*; both plants are similar in appearance. Both come in green form (Irish) and golden green form (Scotch). *Sagina subulata* more common in nurseries. Not a true moss; won't grow in deep shade. *Culture:* Zones A–H, 5–10; full sun or partial shade; will take light foot traffic; small to medium-size areas; moderate growth rate. Useful to fill in between steppingstones. Set pieces from flats 6 inches apart. If plantings form humps, cut out chunks or strips and press humps down. Plant needs good soil, ample water. *Foliage and flowers:* Foliage fine and mosslike. Green form a clean light color; gold forms range from greenish yellow to very yellow. White flowers either solitary (in *Sagina*) or in clusters (in *Arenaria*). See photo on page 91.

St. Johnswort. See Hypericum

Sand strawberry. See Fragaria

SANTOLINA. Profusely flowering gray or green-leafed plants. Good as wide borders behind annuals, or for small to medium-size areas.

S. chamaecyparissus. Lavender cotton. *Culture:* Zones A–H, 7–10; full sun; no foot traffic; small to medium-size areas; moderate to fast growth rate. Set plants 3 feet apart. To keep contained, prune to 1 foot tall; replace if plants become woody. (Easy to grow from cuttings.) May die to ground in coldest areas, but roots survive and resume growth. *Foliage and flowers:* Dense, narrow, woolly gray leaves finely divided on brittle woody stems. Yellow buttonlike flowers appear in summer on unclipped plants.

S. virens. *Culture:* Same as *S. chamaecyparissus.* Grows faster, tolerates more water. Fire retardant. *Foliage and flowers:* Narrow, finely divided, green leaves with striking texture. Creamy chartreuse flowers. See photo on page 51.

SARCOCOCCA humilis (*S. hookeriana humilis*). Evergreen shrub with nearly invisible, very fragrant flowers. *Culture:* Zones B–D, F–H, 6–10; partial to full shade, will take sun in cool-summer areas, no foot traffic; good in small to medium-size areas; slow growth rate; likes rich soil with much organic matter. Set plants 2–3 feet apart. *Foliage and flowers:* Plants grow to 1½ feet tall, spread by runners to 8 feet or more. Leaves glossy, very dark green, oval, pointed, to 3 inches long, closely set on branches. Tiny, white fragrant flowers hidden in foliage in early spring, followed by glossy, blue black fruit.

SATUREJA douglasii (*Micromeria chamissonis*). Yerba buena. Creeping perennial best for cool or shaded wild areas. May be hard to locate. Leaf fragrance varies from mint to blueberry to turpentine. Dried leaves make pleasant tea. *Culture:* Zones A–D, F–H, 7–9; sun along coast, partial shade inland; will stand very light foot traffic; best in small areas or in patches over large areas; moderate to fast growth rate; needs rich, moist soil. Set nursery plants 12 inches apart. *Foliage and flowers:* Rounded, 1-inch long, dusty green, scallop-edged leaves fairly dense on long trailing stems that can spread to 3 feet, rooting as they grow. Height varies from flat to several inches. Tiny, white or lavender-tinted flowers bloom April–September. May reseed itself.

SAXIFRAGA stolonifera (*S. sarmentosa*). Strawberry geranium. Perennial best in climates with fairly cool summers. *Culture:* Zones A–D, F–H, 7–10; partial or full shade; no foot traffic; best in small areas; fast growing; needs constant moisture. Good companion for azaleas, other shade-loving plants. Set divisions 12 inches apart or nursery plants 18 inches apart. *Foliage and flowers:* Round, white-veined leaves, pink underneath, to 4 inches across on creeping plant with strawberrylike runners. Open clusters of white flowers, 1 inch across, on stems to 2 feet tall.

Scotch heather. See Calluna

Scotch moss. See Sagina

SEDUM. Stonecrop. Fleshy-leafed succulent perennials, some hardy in considerable cold, others tender. All have clusters of small, starlike flowers. Sometimes a patch will die back spoiling the uniform appearance. See photos on page 91.

S. acre. Goldmoss sedum. *Culture:* Zones A–H, 4–10; full sun; no foot traffic; leaves soft and easily crushed; best in small to medium-size areas; moderate to fast growth rate. Set nursery plants 12 inches apart, or use stem cuttings set 6 inches apart. Keep moist in dry seasons. *Foliage and flowers:* Upright branchlets 2–5 inches tall on trailing branches that root where they touch. Tiny light green leaves; clustered yellow flowers mid to late spring.

S. album (*S. brevifolium*). *Culture:* Same as *S. acre. Foliage and flowers:* Creeping evergreen to 6 inches tall. Fleshy, ½-inch-long leaves, light to medium green with red tints. White or pinkish white flowers.

S. anglicum. *Culture:* Same as *S. acre. Foliage and flowers:* Low spreading plants to 4 inches tall. Dark green fleshy leaves ⅛ inch long. Spring flowers pinkish white.

S. brevifolium. *Culture:* Zones D, F–H, 9, 10; otherwise, same as *S. acre.* Plants sunburn in hot dry places. Need good drainage. Best in small patches in entryways or in rock gardens. *Foliage and flowers:* Slowly spreading plants to 3 inches tall. Tiny gray white leaves, flushed red. Flowers pinkish or white.

S. confusum (often sold as *S. amecamecanum*). Mexican sedum. *Culture:* Zones D, F–H, 9, 10; otherwise same as *S. acre. Foliage and flowers:* Spreading branching plant 6–8 inches tall; bright yellow green leaves ¾ inch long. Clusters of yellow flowers in spring, summer. May die back in hot weather or with excess moisture.

S. dasyphyllum. *Culture:* Zones D, F–H, 9, 10; otherwise, same as *S. acre.* Best in small areas. *Foliage and flowers:* Plants to 2 inches tall with tiny, closely packed, soft blue green leaves. Spring flowers white.

S. lineare (*S. sarmentosum*). *Culture:* Same as *S. acre. Foliage and flowers:* Trailing rooting stems to 1 foot long. Light green, narrow leaves. Profuse yellow flowers in spring and early summer.

S. moranense. *Culture:* Zones D–H, 9, 10; otherwise same as *S. acre.* Best in small areas. *Foliage and flowers:* Spreading, many-branched plants to 3 inches tall. Small, cylindrical, fleshy, light green leaves turn reddish in sun or cold weather. White flowers sparse.

S. oaxacanum. *Culture:* Zones D–H, 9, 10; otherwise, same as *S. acre.* Will take poor soil. *Foliage and flowers:* Spreading rooting stems a few inches tall with tiny, gray green leaves. Yellow flowers in spring.

S. reflexum (*S. altissimum*). *Culture:* Zones D–H, 9, 10; otherwise, same as *S. acre. Foliage and flowers:* Fairly tall (to 16 inches) spreading plants. Blue gray leaves closely set on stems. Small yellow flowers.

S. rubrotinctum (*S. guatemalense*). Pork and beans. *Culture:* Zones D, F–H, 9, 10; otherwise, same as *S. acre.* Best in small areas. *Foliage and flowers:* Plants 6–8 inches tall. Green leaves with reddish brown tops resemble jelly beans, often entirely bronze red in sunny areas. Flowers reddish yellow.

S. sediforme. *Culture:* Zones D–H, 9, 10; otherwise, same as *S. acre. Foliage and flowers:* Narrow, blue gray leaves to 1½ inches long, closely set on stems; spreading, up to 16 inches high. Flowers greenish white.

S. spathulifolium. *Culture:* Same as *S. acre. Foliage and flowers:* Leaves spoon shaped, blue green with purple tinges, in rosettes on short trailing stems. Light yellow flowers in spring, summer. Varieties are 'Purpureum', purple leaves, and 'Cape Blanco'.

S. spurium. *Culture:* Same as *S. acre. Foliage and flowers:* Large, thick, dark green leaves with bronze tints on trailing stems. Pink summer flowers on erect stems 4–5 inches long. 'Dragon's Blood' has bronzy leaves with rosy red bloom.

Serbian bellflower. See Campanula

Shore juniper. See Juniperus

Snow-in-summer. See Cerastium

SOLEIROLIA soleirolii (*Helxine soleirolii*). Baby's tears. Tiny-leafed mosslike perennial for shady areas. *Culture:* Zone D–H, 9, 10; partial or full shade; occasional foot traffic, stems easily injured, but aggressive growth habit quickly repairs damage; best in small to medium-size areas; fast growing. Freezes to black mush in hard frosts, but comes back quickly. Roots easily from pieces of stem; can become invasive pest. Set nursery plants or cuttings 12 inches apart. *Foliage and flowers:* Tiny round leaves crowd in lush mounding carpet to 4 inches high. Flowers insignificant. See photos on pages 45, 50.

Speedwell. See Veronica

Sprenger asparagus. See Asparagus

Star jasmine. See Trachelospermum

Stonecrop. See Sedum

Strawberry geranium. See Saxifraga

Sunrose. See Helianthemum

Sweet violet. See Viola

Sweet woodruff. See Galium

SYMPHORICARPOS mollis. Creeping snowberry. Deciduous western native for shady areas. Not a dense cover, but natural looking for woodsy garden. May grow very flat or fairly erect, depending on location and available light. *Culture:* Zones B–H, 6–9; partial or full shade; no foot traffic; best in small to medium-size areas; fast growing when established. Set nursery plants 18 inches apart; set rooted cuttings 12 inches apart. Don't overwater in summer. *Foliage and flowers:* Small, round, dull green to grayish green leaves on long stems that may be fairly woody. Leaves either sparse or dense, depending on light. Clusters of tiny pinkish flowers, may be followed by showy snow-white berries that hang on into winter.

T

Tamarix juniper. See Juniperus

Teaberry. See Gaultheria

TEUCRIUM chamaedrys. Germander. Tough, evergreen, shrubby plant especially good in hot, dry climates. *Culture:* Zones A–H, 5–10; full sun; no foot traffic; either small or large areas; fast growing. Thrives in poor and rocky soils, sun and heat; will take regular watering only if drainage is good. Set plants 2 feet apart, or 18 inches for dwarf form 'Prostratum'. Shear once or twice a year to keep neat, force side branching. *Foliage and flowers:* Toothed, dark green leaves to ¾-inch long densely cover erect stems to 1 foot tall; plants spread to 2 feet wide, with many upright stems. Red purple or white flowers in loose spikes during summer. Variety 'Prostratum', 4–6 inches tall, spreads to 3 feet. See photo on page 51.

Thyme. See Thymus

THYMUS. Thyme. Shrubby perennials with usually heavily scented foliage. See photos on pages 45, 92.

T. herba-barona. Caraway-scented thyme. *Culture:* Zones A–H, 4–10; full sun; some foot traffic; small to medium-size areas; fast growing when established. Set nursery plants 6–12 inches apart, cuttings 6 inches or closer in fall or spring. Don't overwater or overfertilize. Plant likes well-drained, fairly dry soil. Will stand neglect. Control plants by clipping growing tips. *Foliage and flowers:* Flat mat of dark green, ¼-inch long leaves with caraway fragrance. Rose pink flowers in headlike clusters in spring.

T. lanuginosus. Woolly thyme. *Culture:* Same as *T. herba-barona. Foliage and flowers:* Undulating mat, 2–3 inches high. Dense, tiny, gray woolly leaves. May have pinkish flowers in spring.

T. serpyllum. Mother-of-thyme, creeping thyme. *Culture:* Same as *T. herba-barona.* Use as filler between steppingstones or in small areas. *Foliage and flowers:* Creeping mat to 6 inches high; can be clipped shorter. Tiny, dark green, roundish, aromatic leaves. Headlike clusters of small, purplish white summer flowers.

T. s. 'Argenteus'. *Culture:* Same as *T. herba-barona. Foliage:* Leaves variegated with silver.

T. s. vulgaris. *Culture:* Same as *T. herba-barona. Foliage:* Lemon-scented foliage.

TIARELLA cordifolia. Allegheny foam flower. Perennial. Striking eastern native for moist woodland settings. *Culture:* Zones B, F, 4–9; partial to full shade; no foot traffic; best in small to medium-size areas; fast growing when established; likes moist, somewhat acid soil. Set plants 12 inches apart. *Foliage and flowers:* Leaves lobed and maplelike to about 4 inches long, carried on 4–8-inch leaf stalks; both covered with downy hairs. Leaves turn bronzy red in fall. In May, spikes of small, frothy white flowers.

TOLMIEA menziesii. Piggy-back plant. Western native perennial for shady areas. Grown mainly for foliage. *Culture:* Zones B (all but coldest)–D, E (warmest parts)–H, 8, 9; partial to full shade; no foot traffic; best in small to medium-size areas; moderate growth rate; needs ample moisture, will tolerate wet soil. Set nursery plants 12 inches apart. *Foliage and flowers:* Hairy, 5-inch-wide leaves are slightly lobed, very densely packed, rising from ground on leaf stalks up to 12 inches long. Tiny new plants form where stalk joins leaf. Each new plant will root where it touches moist soil. Rather insignificant, tiny, red brown flowers on long spikes.

TRACHELOSPERMUM jasminoides. Star jasmine, Confederate jasmine. Not a true jasmine (see also *Jasminum*, page 79), but offers powerful perfume. Withstands humidity of Gulf coast as well as dry heat of Southwest. *Culture:* Zones D–H, 9, 10; full sun or light shade (must have shade in hottest areas); no foot traffic; small or large areas; slow to start, then fairly fast growing. Keep stems pinned down or trimmed to keep plants low. Fertilize in spring, late summer. Keep well watered. Set nursery plants 1½–3 feet apart. *Foliage and flowers:* Glossy, dark green, pointed leaves to 3 inches long with light green new growth. Plants woody, to 2 feet tall, spreading to 5 feet. Clusters of small, white, star-shaped flowers that release strong fragrance after sundown in June, July. See photos on pages 46, 92.

TRADESCANTIA fluminensis. Wandering Jew. Attractive perennial for mild climates. *Culture:* Zones E (warmer parts)–H, 9, 10; partial shade; no foot traffic; best in small to medium-size areas; withstands wet soil. Set cuttings or nursery plants 12–18 inches apart. *Foliage and flowers:* Succulent stems with swollen joints where pointed 2½-inch-long leaves attach. Leaf color ranges from dark green through red-backed to variegated green and white or green and yellow. Leaf color better with some sun. Plants under 4 inches tall, but spread widely, rooting as they go, with many branches. Tiny, white or pinkish flowers at stem tips.

Trailing African daisy. See Osteospermum

Tussock bellflower. See Campanula

V

VACCINIUM vitis-idaea. Lingonberry. Rare evergreen plant for moist cool areas with acid soil. Source of cranberrylike fruit used by Swedish cooks for perserves. *Culture:* Zones B, C, 3–5; sun or partial shade; needs cool summers, acid, moist soil; no foot traffic; best in small areas; slow growth rate. Set nursery plants 12 inches apart. *Foliage, flowers, and fruit:* Plants to 1 foot tall, spread to 3 feet by underground runners. Dark green leaves 1 inch long. White or pinkish flowers in May. Edible, translucent looking red berries are good cooked

like cranberries. *V. v. minus* a smaller form. See photo on page 50.

VANCOUVERIA planipetala (*V. parviflora*). Inside-out flower. Perennial with good flower display for woodsy shade. Look in nurseries that specialize in western native plants. *Culture:* Zones B, D(warmest parts), F, 7–9; part to full shade; no foot traffic; best in small areas under trees; moderate growth rate. Set nursery plants 12 inches apart. May be deciduous in cold-winter areas. *Foliage and flowers:* Plants to 2 feet tall with light to medium green leaflets, shallowly lobed, 1½ inches long and wide. Sprays of 25–50 tiny white flowers in May, June; the flower parts bend backward, giving inside-out appearance. See photo on page 50.

VERBENA. Perennial plant with brilliant flower color for hot, dry summer climates. Elsewhere, treat as an annual; plants cover rapidly. Mildews in humid climates or if overwatered. Not generally successful east of the Rockies. See photos on page 93.

V. hybrida (*V. hortensis*). Garden verbena. *Culture:* Zones A–H; full sun; no foot traffic; small to medium-size areas; fast growing. Drought resistant; water deeply, then let soil dry out. Set nursery plants 2 feet apart. Cut back heavily in winter or early spring. *Foliage and flowers:* Plants, 6–12 inches tall, branching and spreading to 3 feet across. Large, oblong, gray green, toothed leaves. Abundant flowers in flat clusters 2–3 inches wide. Colors are white, pink, bright red, purple, blue, and combinations; named varieties available in specific colors.

V. peruviana (*V. chamaedryfolia*). *Culture:* Zones D–H; otherwise, same as *V. hybrida. Foliage and flowers:* Plants spread rapidly to form very flat mat. Neat, small, closely set grayish leaves. Abundant flat flower clusters with white tubes, spreading scarlet lobes. Hybrids in other colors: 'Appleblossom', 'Cherry Pink', 'Princess Gloria' in salmon; many purplish and red forms; a pure white form.

VERONICA. Speedwell. Perennial. Some nursery plants sold as *Veronica* now grouped with *Hebe* (see page 73). Below are low spreading creepers with abundant tiny bloom for small sunny areas.

V. pectinata. *Culture:* Zones A–H, 4–10; full sun; no foot traffic; best in small areas; moderate growth rate. Set plants 6 inches apart. *Foliage and*

(Continued on page 95)

ROSMARINUS officinalis

Popular, drought-tolerant herb that will trail over steep banks or walls or form low mound. Narrow, dark green leaves with blue flowers most of winter. (See page 88.)

SAGINA subulata

Ground-hugging, mosslike, carpeting ground cover with bright green and golden green forms. Irish moss shown here likes full sun, will take light foot traffic. (See page 88.)

SEDUM

Large family of fleshy-leafed, succulent perennials; all have clusters of small, star-shaped flowers (right). Green leaves may turn reddish in sun or cold weather. In full bloom (above), sedum ground cover makes a colorful display. Yellow flower form is Sedum album, white form is Sedum brevifolium. (See page 89.)

THYMUS herba-barona

Easy-to-grow ground cover that can handle some foot traffic and usually has fragrant leaves. Thymus herba-barona with dark green, caraway-scented foliage (above) makes good low cover that can stand some neglect. Headlike clusters of rose pink flowers (left) bloom in spring. (See pages 89–90.)

TRACHELOSPERMUM jasminoides

Good cover for warm, mild-winter climates; can take humidity of Gulf coast or dry heat of Southwest. The woody-stemmed, spreading plants form a cover (above) that stays about 2 feet tall. Foliage (left) is dark green, glossy, with light green new growth; clusters of tiny, white, star-shaped flowers give off strong fragrance after sundown in summer. (See page 90.)

VERBENA

Perennial plant grown for its brilliant flower color in areas with hot, dry summer climates. In other areas, these covers are used as annuals. Verbena hybrida (left) likes full sun, is drought tolerant, has gray green, toothed foliage, abundant flowers in flat clusters, available in white, pink, bright red, purple, blue, and combinations. Verbena peruviana (above) spreads to form very flat mat. Flower clusters have white tubes with spreading scarlet lobes. (See page 90.)

VIBURNUM davidii

For shady areas with acid soil, these small, spreading evergreen shrubs make good companion plants for azaleas, ferns. Used in a mass (left), foliage overlaps for dense cover. Leaves (above) are dark green, deeply veined, 3 to 6 inches long. White flower clusters, not showy, are followed by metallic turquoise blue fruits if several shrubs are planted. Design: R. David Adams. (See page 95.)

VINCA minor
Frequently used ground cover for partly shaded areas. Planted in a landscape (above), vinca spreads and mounds for a solid cover. Plant (right) has glossy, dark green, pointed leaves on trailing stems. Lavender blue, white, or deep blue star-shaped flowers appear in spring, fall. (See page 95.)

VIOLA hederacea
Shade-loving perennial cover for small areas spreads by creeping stolons. Foliage is small, kidney-shaped. Tiny, pansylike flowers in white, blue, or combinations bloom in summer. (See page 95.)

flowers: Prostrate mats with creeping stems that root at joints. Roundish ½-inch leaves with scalloped or deeply cut edges. Profuse flowers in 5–6-inch spikes, deep blue with white centers.

V. prostrata (V. rupestris). *Culture:* Zones B–H, 6–10; otherwise, same as *V. pectinata. Foliage and flowers:* Tufted, hairy stems, some erect. Leaves to ¾ inch long. Flower stems to 8 inches, topped with short cluster of pale blue flowers.

V. repens. *Culture:* Zones B–H, 6–10; otherwise, same as *V. pectinata.* Good cover for small bulbs. *Foliage and flowers:* Shining, ½-inch-long green leaves on prostrate stems give mosslike effect. Tiny lavender or white flowers in small clusters in spring.

VIBURNUM davidii. Small, spreading, evergreen shrub for shady areas. Good companion plant for azaleas, ferns. *Culture:* Zones B–D, F–H, 7–10; partial shade; no foot traffic; good in small to medium-size areas; slow growth rate; needs acid soil. Set plants 18 inches apart. *Foliage, flowers, and fruit:* To 3 feet tall, often lower, spreading to 4 feet wide. Deeply veined, dark green leaves 3–6 inches long. White flowers from pinkish red buds form clusters to 3 inches wide; not showy. Fruits metallic turquoise blue. Several plants needed for berry production. See photos on page 93.

VINCA. Periwinkle, myrtle. Evergreen perennials. See photos on pages 46, 94.

V. major. *Culture:* Zones B (all but coldest)–H, 8–10; partial shade, sun if watered generously, full shade in hot areas; very light foot traffic; either small or large areas; fast growing. Set plants or rooted cuttings 12–18 inches apart. Shear close to ground occasionally to bring on fresh growth. *Foliage and flowers:* Rather erect stems make thick mats that can mound to 2 feet tall. Large, glossy, dark green pointed leaves to 3 inches long. White and yellow variegated leaf forms also common. Lavender blue, star-shaped flowers to 2 inches across in spring, summer; rather scattered.

V. minor. *Culture:* Zones A–H, 4–10; otherwise, same as *V. major. Foliage and flowers:* In appearance, miniature form of *V. major.* Trailing stems very flat or mounding to 12 inches high. Leaves more oblong on shorter stalks. One-inch star-shaped flowers in lavender blue, white, deep blue in spring and fall.

Vine Hill manzanita. See Arctostaphylos

VIOLA. Violet. Shade-loving perennials are good cover for small shaded areas. See photos on pages 45, 94.

V. hederacea. Australian violet. *Culture:* Zones D, F–H, 9, 10; full sun in coastal areas, partial shade in warmer climates, full shade in desert and hot-summer areas; no foot traffic; best in small areas; fast growing. Set nursery plants 6 inches apart. Plant needs rich moist soil. Goes dormant at 30° F. *Foliage and flowers:* Creeping plants, spreading by stolons. Small kidney-shaped leaves. Pansylike flowers to ¾ inch across, white or blue, fading to white at tips in summer.

V. odorata. Sweet violet. *Culture:* Zones A–H, 6–10; otherwise, same as *V. hederacea. Foliage and flowers:* Long tufted runners root at joints. Dark green, heart-shaped leaves toothed on margins. Short-spurred fragrant flowers hidden in leaves. Colors vary: 'Royal Robe', deep blue, large; 'Marie Louise', double white or bluish lavender; 'Royal Elk', violet, single; 'Charm', white, grows in clumps; 'Rosina', pink.

V. priceana. Confederate violet. *Culture:* Zones A–H, 6–10; otherwise, same as *V. hederacea.* Self sows readily. Best in woodland gardens. *Foliage and flowers:* Leaves to 5 inches wide, somewhat heart shaped. Flat-faced pansylike flowers, ½–¾ inch across, white, blue veined.

Violet. See Viola

Virginia creeper. See Parthenocissus

Vittadinia. See Erigeron

Wall rockcress. See Arabis

Wandering Jew. See Tradescantia

Wavy-leafed plantain lily. See Hosta

White cup. See Nierembergia

Wild ginger. See Asarum

Wild lilac. See Ceanothus

Wild strawberry. See Fragaria

Winter creeper. See Euonymus

Wintergreen. See Gaultheria

Wire vine. See Muehlenbeckia

Woolly grevillea. See Grevillea

Woolly thyme. See Thymus

Woolly yarrow. See Achillea

XANTHORHIZA simplicissima. Yellow root. Eastern woodland deciduous shrubby plant for moist soils. *Culture:* Zones B, F, 5–10; either sun or shade; no foot traffic; good in medium to large areas; fast growing. Set plants or rooted cuttings 2 feet apart. *Foliage and flowers:* Fairly uniform cover to 2 feet high. Spreads by suckers from spreading roots. Green leaves divided into 5 leaflets, often lobed and divided, turning orange in fall. Tiny purplish flowers appear before leaves in early spring.

Yarrow. See Achillea

Yellow root. See Xanthorhiza

Yerba buena. See Satureja

ZAUSCHNERIA. California fuchsia, hummingbird flower. Shrubby perennial. For hot dry areas similar to its native California hills. Long, red, tubular flowers and gray leaves are striking, but plant only covers sparsely. *Culture:* Zones B–D, F–H, not generally successful east of the Rockies; full sun; no foot traffic; best in small areas or scattered among larger plantings; moderate growth; needs a dry summer. Set plants 24 inches apart. *Foliage and flowers:* Two common forms, both with small clusters of striking red flowers and narrow gray leaves are Z. *californica,* woody, erect, arching, to 2 feet tall; Z. *cana,* sprawling with denser foliage.

ZOYSIA tenuifolia. Korean grass. Grows in tough lumpy clumps; won't take mowing. *Culture:* Zones D–H, 9, 10; full sun to medium shade; best in small to medium-size areas; fast growing. Hardy to 10° F., but turns brown with first frost, remaining brown until early spring. Plant pieces from flats 8 inches apart. *Foliage:* Rich fine-textured green grass with a lumpy, undulating growth pattern.

Climate Zone Maps, pages 42–43

Sunset
Proof-of-Purchase
ISBN 0-376-03507-2

Index

This index gives page references for lawns and general garden information only. To find an individual ground cover description, look up the plant name in the alphabetical listing, pages 56–95.

Photographers

William Aplin: 76 top right. **Glenn M. Christiansen:** 52, 61 top right. **Gerald R. Fredrick:** 33 top and lower left, 35, 36 lower, 46 top left, 47 top, 50 center right, 51 lower center, 62 top right, 68 lower left, 69 lower right, 77 top left and right, 78 lower, 84 lower left and right, 85 lower right, 86 top and lower, 91 lower right, 93 top left, 94 lower. **Steve W. Marley:** 61 top left, 62 top left and lower right, 64 top right and lower, 67 top right, 77 lower left and right, 78 top right, 91 top left and right, 92 top left and right, lower left. **Ells Marugg:** 33 lower right, 36 top, 45 lower, 46 lower, 47 lower, 49 top, 50 top, center left, lower, 61 lower, 62 lower left and center, 63, 64 top left, center left, 67 top left, lower left and right, 68 top left and right, lower right, 69 top right, lower left, 70, 75, 76 lower left and right, 78 top left, 83 lower, 84 top left and right, 85 top, lower left, 86 center, 91 lower left, 92 lower right, 93 top right, lower left and right, 94 top, center, back cover, lower. **Norman A. Plate:** 34, 48, 49 lower, 51 lower left and right, 69 top left, 76 top left, 83 top, back cover, top. **Bill Ross:** 45 top, 46 top right. **Bob Smaus:** 64 center right. **Peter O. Whiteley:** 51 top.